Classic Jeeps

Classic Jeeps

THE JEEP FROM WORLD WAR II TO THE PRESENT DAY

John Carroll

Photographs by Garry Stuart

MBI Publishing Company

This edition first published in 2000 by MBI Publishing Company,
729 Prospect Avenue, PO Box 1, Osceola, WI 54020-0001 USA

MBI Publishing Company books are also available at discounts in bulk quantity for industrial or sales-
promotional use. For details write to Special Sales Manager at Motorbooks International Wholesalers
& Distributors, 729 Prospect Avenue, PO Box 1, Osceola, WI 54020-0001 USA.

Library of Congress Cataloging-in-Publication Data Available

ISBN 0-7603-0894-2

Printed in Spain

Credits
Editor Phil Hunt
Designers Richard Mason, John Heritage
All photographs by Garry Stuart
Film set: SX Composing Ltd, England
Reproduction: Studio Technology

Acknowledgements
Both the author and the photographer are indebted to all the owners of the Jeeps photographed for
this book as well as the organisers of the Ouray Jeep Jamboree and Rachel Dunham at
Chrysler Jeep Imports UK.

The author is further indebted to Kevin Hawkins for an unforgettable flatfender Jeep-ride up the
Lion's Back in Moab, Utah, to Neville Langley for hours of help with a flatfender Jeep in England and
to the boy who, in 1943, sat on a gate in a Cheshire, England lane and waved to a convoy of US
Army trucks. He wouldn't have known then that it was part of Patton's Third US Army but in 1999
he, my Dad, still happily remembers how all the G.I.s waved back.

This book is respectfully dedicated to Willie and Joe and all the other Dogfaces.

Jeep is a trademark of Chrysler-Daimler

Additional captions
page 1: Dan Mick's Wrangler
pages 2-3: A CJ-5 at the Ouray Jeep Jamboree, 1998
pages 4-5: Tony Sudds' Bantam BRC and Ford GP
pages 6-7: Barry Redman's 1947 CJ-2A
pages 8-9: The Lion's Back, Moab, Utah
page 10: A TJ Wrangler in action

Endpapers: A TJ Wrangler at the Ouray Jeep Jamboree, 1998

CONTENTS

591 BFR

INTRODUCTION

Left: The instantly recognizable radiator grille of the Jeep, in this case a CJ-2A, one of the classic flatfenders.

THIS JEEP BOOK DIFFERS from others about Jeeps because within its pages the reader will not find a dry model-by-model and year-by-year history of the various vehicles to have carried the Jeep brand name. They are simply mass-produced working trucks made from iron and steel like other automobiles. While the term 'iron horse' may have been coined for high-stepping Harley Davidsons, someone described the Jeep as a 'mechanical mule' many years ago, and it is a wholly appropriate analogy. The Jeep was nothing more than a mechanical mule designed to help win the new war and then be cast aside with the debris of it. James Jones defined this new type of warfare: "Modern war was not a football game. And modern war was not man against man – if it ever had been. It was machine against machine. It was industry against industry. And we had the best machine. Our industry was better than their industry. But men had to die or be maimed to prove it. men had to die at the wheels or triggers of the machines."

What made the Jeep great was that, in the manner of the mule, it was tougher than anyone expected and that when driven with sufficient panache, and not a little desperation, the Jeep seemed capable of the impossible. At a time when cars generally featured curved fenders the angular Jeep looked good; its austere but modern design made even the lowliest white trash GI in his tailored uniform look like a Hollywood film star while driving a Jeep. It's little wonder that the GIs left broken hearts behind everywhere when they went off to fight and die in Normandy and the Pacific. So the legend of the Jeep was born and in every theater of war, from the beaches of Normandy and the mud of the Belgian Ardennes to the jungles of Burma and the sands of Iwo Jima, the Jeep endeared itself to the soldiers of the Allied armies. Fighting machine, ambulance, message carrier, mechanical mule, recreational vehicle; the Willys Jeep was all of them and more. It was the transport of soldiers and of generals of many nations, in all types of terrain and in all theaters of operations. By the end of the war General Eisenhower was to comment that the Jeep was amongst the tools that helped America win its war, along with machines such as the amphibious truck, Douglas DC3 aeroplane and the bulldozer. None of these machines was actually designed for combat use, but instead to ease the logistics of a mobile war.

Before World War Two, Willys was never one of the big auto-makers like Ford or Chevrolet. Having said that, as any street-rodder knows, it did build some highly regarded automobiles, most notably the

'33 and '41 coupes. These models were often the basis of the later gassers that turned fast times in the quarter mile. However, this book isn't about drag racing, but looks at a road much less traveled by the internal combustion engine. Because Willys existed in the shadow of the major manufacturers it's easy to imagine its engineers' excitement at the prospect of building a new type of vehicle, especially one that might conceivably 'bring home the bacon.' The new vehicle had the potential to put Willys' name up there with those of Ford and Chevrolet. The US Army Quartermaster Corps had issued the specification for a new quarter-ton 4x4 and the race was on. Bantam, Ford and Willys were among the contenders and there was even interest from the likes of Minneapolis-Moline, an established tractor maker. It might be true that Karl Probst, who worked for Bantam, devised the vehicle that became known as the Jeep and it might be equally true that Ford's capacity for mass production

ensured massive and standardized production, but history records that it was Willys who made the 'Jeep'.

Historical documents cannot conclusively prove the origins of the name 'Jeep' – more than half a century after the first model was built its origins are so imprecise as not to be the dust dry facts of history but the altogether more glorious stuff of legends. For example, 'Eugene the Jeep' was one of the diverse characters in the Popeye cartoon strip and the designation 'GP' can easily be abbreviated into Jeep. Ever since the interest in Jeeps mushroomed, worthy historians have argued about the exact origins of its name. The fact that the debate still rages is of little consequence. The doubt over the Jeep's origins reflects the uncertainty of the times in which the Jeep was conceived. What really matters when it comes to Jeeps is that the tires hum on a dirt road and the transfer case whines when four-wheel drive is engaged. Move 'em out.

Left: *The styling of the Jeep has evolved over the decades so that in a current model the design cues of the originals (**right**) can clearly be seen.*

Above: *The second versions of the vehicles designed by Bantam and Ford to fulfil the military specification, the BRC and GP, left and right respectively.*
Inset right: *Eugene the Jeep, the Popeye character who some say the 4x4 is named after.*

"A marked improvement in cross-country mobility of tactical vehicles has resulted from the development of the all-wheel drive."

GENERAL GEORGE C. MARSHALL. REPORT ON THE ARMY.
JULY 1 1939 TO JUNE 30 1943.

WAR BABIES

WORLD WAR TWO started in Europe in September 1939 when German Panzers rolled into Poland with a new form of war – the blitzkrieg or 'lightning war.' In response to this development President Roosevelt made an emergency proclamation on September 8 1939. The proclamation authorized an increase in size of both the regular army and the National Guard. The War Department was also authorized to spend an additional $12 million on motor transport. In May 1940 additional money for the army was recommended by the President to Congress on two occasions. Despite the fact that the US was not directly involved in the war at this time, the total approved was in excess of two billion dollars. Holland fell to the German blitzkrieg in May 1940. France fell to the same aggressors in June 1940 and in the same month the US Army Quartermaster Corps issued a specification for a lightweight vehicle capable of carrying men and equipment across rough terrain. It invited 130 different manufacturers to build prototypes and submit them for testing after which a contract for 70 pre-production models would be awarded to some makers. Initially only two manufacturers showed sufficient interest to build prototypes, namely Willys Overland and American Bantam, both of whom were in some financial difficulty at the time. The vehicles presented for testing were the Willys Quad and the Bantam Reconnaissance Car (BRC). The period allowed for the various manufacturers to design and build their prototypes was only 75 days. Many manufacturers thought the deadline was too short and felt they could not hope to build anything to the overall specification with a maximum weight of only 590 kg. The Willys' prototype was late and Bantam received a contract for 70 vehicles after considerable testing of its machine – the Bantam 40BRC – at Camp Holabird in Baltimore, Maryland.

At the Bantam Car Company in Butler, Pennsylvania, President Francis H. Fenn contacted Karl K. Probst, a freelance auto designer. The latter agreed to take on design work for Bantam in mid-July once Bantam had received its bid documents from the military for the project. Fenn, Probst and Harold Crist drew up a specification and spoke to component suppliers. Spicer axles – as on the Studebaker Champion – and transfer cases were to be used, as were Warner transmission, instruments from the Bantam car and, after deciding Bantam's own engine was too small, an 1835cc side-valve Continental engine. With components chosen and dimensions noted, Probst was able to draw up a design and within a week of receiving the bid papers Fenn and Probst were able to travel to

Left: *Styling of the quarter-ton 4x4 was austere but wholly functional as evidenced by the means of headlight protection used on Bantam's BRC (Bantam Reconnaissance Car.)*

Camp Holabird, Maryland, to make their submission. Willys' representatives were also there but their project was not as advanced and, in accordance with the terms of the contract, would cost more per vehicle. Bantam was awarded the contract. Official notification was received by Bantam on August 5 1940, meaning that the company had 49 days to get a running prototype to Holabird. Because of the tight schedule the new vehicle was designed with mostly proven technology, including leaf springs, ladder frame chassis and a separate steel body. This became the Model 60, with a rounded radiator grille and curved front fenders. On September 23 Probst and Crist set off to drive the 275 km to Camp Holabird, Fenn following behind in a car loaded with some spares including heavier springs and a different radiator. Once delivered to Camp Holabird the test would begin immediately and the Model 60 had to endure a 30-day test period. The

vehicle withstood the testing and parts that did fail were repairable, resulting in a positive evaluation for the Bantam. The company was given its contract for 70 slightly revised models known as the Model 60 Mark 2. Before these were completed a second contract, for 1,500 vehicles, was awarded to Bantam for the 40BRC. This was the 1940 Bantam Reconnaissance Car, a further modified version of the Model 60 which incorporated features from the Ford prototype including its flat hood.

As noted, Willys-Overland had lost out to Bantam for the initial contract for 70 vehicles because of a 'small print' penalty clause of $5 per day, which made its vehicles more expensive than those of Bantam. Delmar 'Barney' Roos, Willys' Chief Engineer, was anxious to be involved with military vehicle production because Willys-Overland had financial problems and also because he knew that the idea of a light 4x4

Right: *After arduous trials American Bantam received a government contract for 1,500 examples of the BRC in this form.*

was a sound one. Willys-Overland's management were of the opinion that the Bantam prototype would not withstand the 30-day test period so decided to build their version at their own expense.

Willys' engineers were allowed to see the Bantam prototype in action and examine it closely. It is also recorded that both Ford and Willys were given copies of the blueprints for the Bantam machine, a move which was seen by many as the army having doubts about Bantam's ability to build and supply its 4x4 in the numbers in which it would be required. Harold Crist of Bantam was unhappy about this but the Quartermaster Corps argued that as the Bantam machine had been paid for with US Government money they could show it to whoever they wanted. Willys' first quarter-ton 4x4, the Quad, was delivered to Holabird on November 11 1940. It was powered by the company's own Go-Devil engine, a 2199cc side-

valve four cylinder engine that produced 65 bhp. This engine was a refined version of the block that had been introduced in 1933. Much of the Quad was comparable with the Bantam – such as using the same Spicer axles and transfer case – but the Quad was more angular in appearance than the Bantam. On November 13, testing began, comprising of 8000 km on the highway and 8000 km off the highway at Camp Holabird. The off-highway testing involved traversing streams, mud holes, bumps and other natural obstacles.

The Ford Motor Company came to the race later than either Bantam or Willys-Overland and then only after being directly approached in October 1940. Ford built two prototypes of the GP, initially referred to as the Pygmy, and officially described as the Truck 1/4-ton, 4x4, Ford in 1940. Of these two, one was assembled with a body manufactured by Ford while the second had a body made by Budd, a steel pressings com-

Right: *Bantams used a Spicer transfer case which, through use of the two smaller gear levers, enabled four-wheel drive and low range to be selected.*

Below: *The Bantam BRC was fitted with the instruments from the civilian Bantam car of the time. A temperature gauge, ammeter, oil pressure gauge and fuel gauge enabled the driver to check on the engine's functions*

pany. Under the flat hood was a modified 1966cc four cylinder Fordson 9N tractor engine coupled to a three-speed Model A Ford gearbox and proprietary Spicer transfer box. Noted strengths of the Ford prototype were the useable space of the flat hood as well as driver comfort and convenience. Unlike the Budd-bodied Pygmy, Ford's own design put the headlamps behind the radiator grille where they were less susceptible to damage, and gave the vehicle a lower overall profile.

Ford also developed the hinged mountings that allowed the lights to be swivelled to illuminate the engine for field maintenance, this becoming a standard feature on the MB/GPW models. The testing of the prototypes at Camp Holabird was thorough and included high- and low-speed running both on and off road. The tests showed that the Ford GP was prone to overheating, that the transmission jammed in gear on occasions and that the track rod in front of the axle was vulnerable to damage during off-road use when it came into contact with tree stumps and large rocks. Despite these results, Ford was given a contract for 1,500 vehicles on November 19 1940, just four days before testing was due to begin at Camp Holabird, presumably because any remedial work could easily be incorporated into the production models.

The Ford GP models were manufactured at Ford's Rouge River plant in Dearborn, Michigan. Of this plant, Schuyler Van Duyne said in *Popular Science* magazine in August 1941, "Even Ford which boasts the closest thing to a self-contained industrial plant at

its gigantic Rouge [River] works calls upon many outside suppliers and, like General Motors, buys from every state in the country." Examples of subcontracting companies included Budd, who made steel pressings, and Kelsey-Hayes, who made wheels. Ford charged the US Government $975 per GP but would discount the unit price by $50 if payment was settled within 30 days of supply. The first 400 GPs were scheduled for delivery on March 10 1941, with the remainder to be delivered within a few weeks. Willys-Overland received its order for 1,500 vehicles on

December 3 1940, the vehicles redesignated as the Willys MA. Of the 1,500, 49 were to have four-wheel steering as well as four-wheel drive. The MAs were $959 each less 1% for early settlement.

While all this testing was ongoing, events were moving on apace on the world's stage. Considerable debate took place in the US about supporting the nations still fighting the German forces. The need for the United States to have its own defense force suddenly became more urgent following the signing by Germany, Italy and Japan, on September 27 1940, of an agreement to protect the 'new order' in Europe and Asia. This agreement, thinly disguised as a defensive alliance, was perceived as a threat to the United States. According to Edward Riley Stettinius Jr, writing in *Lend-Lease* in 1944, "By December 1940, a majority of the American people, I believe, had made up their minds that it was in our national interest to continue the flow of arms to nations fighting the Axis." Greece and Yugoslavia fell, but on March 11 1941, the Lend Lease Bill became law in the US. Through this tanks, guns, trucks, ships and food would continue to flow to Britain. Under similar agreements this aid would also go to both Russia and China and would later include thousands of Jeeps.

All three companies' machines had the early Jeep 'look'. In a further round of testing it was revealed that all three machines had both strengths and weaknesses. Ford submitted a redesigned prototype, the Ford GP as did Willys, the MA. It was the Willys MA that seemed best overall after further strenuous evalu-

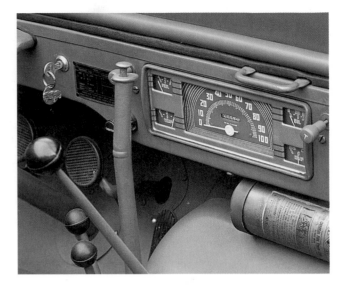

ation tests and in July 1941 Willys was given a contract for 16,000 revised MA models which were referred to as the MB. In the same month George C. Marshall wrote in his *Biennial Report on the Army*, "The mounting experience and lessons learned from the present European conflict dictate a greater propor-

Top, right: *Ford used the instrument panel from its 1941 civilian model pickup truck in the Ford GP.*

Right: *Ford's styling was as austere and functional as that of Willys-Overland and American Bantam although headlights were protected behind the radiator grille.*

tion of mechanized units in our army. From the appropriations provided during fiscal year 1941, procurement has been initiated to cover the various types of combat vehicles, such as light and medium tanks, scout cars and cross-country personnel carriers, in quantities to meet the needs of our protective mobilization plan and, with minor exceptions, sufficient to supply the initial requirements of the augmented force."

That, in the summer of 1941, America was preparing to, at the very least, defend itself was newsworthy, as were the means of the defense. In an article written in *Popular Science* magazine in August 1941 entitled From Cook Stoves to Tanks... They Roll From the Automobile Factories, Schuyler Van Duyne commented on this increasing mechanization. "In addition to 5,900 passenger cars and 27,000 motorcycles, the vehicles ordered are 4,500 quarter-ton scout cars from Ford, Bantam and Willys; 69,000 half-ton pickup and reconnaissance trucks from White." Clearly aware of the fact that each of the three manufacturers had been awarded a contract for 1,500 quarter-ton 4x4 vehicles, he wrote, "Low-silhouette cars can carry crews of three and machine guns. As reconnaissance cars, they are hard to see and hit. They're fast and powerful. Bantam, Willys and Ford are building them." The confusion about the origins of the name Jeep is reflected by the uncertainty of the writers of numerous magazine articles of the time, no doubt perplexed by the varying names, both official and unofficial, used by three different manufacturers. In Motorization and Mechanization, an article in *Popular Science* magazine, David M. Stearns wrote about an armored division, "While the tanks are the heavyweights of the armored force, they are numerically a small part of the vehicles it uses. An armored division has only 290 light and 125 medium tanks while there are 792 2.5-ton trucks, 534 motorcycles and 290 'bantams' plus scout cars and other vehicles in the same division." About the quarter-tonners, he continued, "The 'bantams,' also known to the soldiers as 'beetle-bugs,' 'jeeps,' and by several other names, are stocky little

vehicles only recently adopted for army use." The Bantam was, of course, the 40BRC, while another nickname current at the time was 'Peep.' The President of the Automobile Manufacturers Association, Alvan McCauley, seemed to be referring to Ford's prototypes in Defense on the Assembly Line, an article in *Popular Mechanics* magazine of August 1941: "In June [1941] the US land forces expected to have 190,000 motor vehicles. The new cars form an assorted list – pygmy trucks 80 inches long, seven-ton jobs... Midget trucks are coming from three companies."

The 4,500 Ford GPs, Bantams and Willys MA models were deployed to bases around the US and incorporated into the changing tactics of a rapidly mechanizing US Army. Initially they were used in conjunction with Dodge 4x4s, White Scout Cars and motorcycles, especially by reconnaissance units of the newly formed triangular divisions. Although referred to in magazine articles as being used in conjunction with motorcycles made by Harley Davidson and Indian, the Jeep soon largely superseded the motorcycle for military use. The major exception was military police use. According to A. Wade Wells, "The Jeep revolutionized modern warfare by providing the

Right: *The rear seat of the GP was, like the front seats, comprised of a metal frame and two canvas-covered cushions.*

answer to the problems of supply and maximum mobility." (Hail to the Jeep, 1946.) Once the Willys model was ordered in quantity the Bantam BRC and Ford GP quickly faded into the background.

The contract for 16,000 MAs almost went to Ford simply because the QMC was keen to take advantage of Ford's massive production capability. However, intervention by the Office of Production Management ensured it went to Willys Overland. The 16,000 vehicles were to be supplied with a number of standardized military components fitted including an air filter, electrical suppressors, generator, a military battery, military lights and military instruments. These parts were in use on other military vehicles so simplified the stockholding of spares. Pioneer tools, a jerrycan holder and other standard items were also to be fitted. Demand soon outstripped supply so Ford's massive manufacturing capability was coopted. Edsel Ford accepted a $14.6 million contract on November 10 1941 to manufacture 15,000 Willys MBs to Willys specifications. The Ford-built examples were to be known as GPWs, although parts were completely interchangeable.

The MB and GPWs earned accolades right from the start. Writing about lend-lease supplies to the USSR, Edward Stettinius Jr had this to say of Jeeps: "The Russians early learned the value of our Jeeps too. They had asked for motorcycle sidecars, but as I wrote Ambassador Litvinov late in January 1942, our own army was using Jeeps almost instead of motorcycle sidecars. The Russians decided to try the Jeeps and soon found that our own army had good reason to rely on them. They worked so well in the mire and rough going on the Russian roads that the Red Army quickly asked for more. Since then we have shipped over 20,000 of them to Russia."

An interesting aside concerns these Jeeps. Stettinius, lend-lease administrator between 1941 and 1944, continued by describing an Associated Press correspondent's visit to a Soviet artillery regiment. "He was driven in a Jeep through deep mud and across rough fields to the regimental headquarters.

Between jounces he turned to the Red Army driver and asked him how he liked the tough little car. The driver answered with one word: "Zamechatelno." That is the Russian equivalent for 'swell.'" Willys-Overland had a series of magazine adverts made about its products in action for magazines such as the *Saturday Evening Post*. Each was illustrated with a painted

Above: *The eventual design that was agreed to be the standardized quarter-ton 4x4 was the Willys MB. This was a developed version of the Willys MA.*

illustration and this particular incident was the subject of one of those advertisements.

In the postwar analysis, as early as 1946 A. Wade Wells was able to say of the Jeep's contribution to the war, "Unpretentious beside the monster tank, humble and a little apologetic next to the sleek trim body of a P-38, the Jeep nevertheless accorded more mentions in despatches than any other instrument of war." Given the austere nature of this new vehicle, it has been jokingly suggested that Jeep is an acronym for 'Just Enough Essential Parts.' A number of Jeep variants were later considered and built as prototypes including a six-wheeled Jeep, an armored Jeep, a snow Jeep (in conjunction with Allis Chalmers), weapons-carrying Jeeps, airborne Jeeps and a four-wheel steering Jeep. Some actually went into production. Perhaps the best known of these variants was the amphibious Jeep, nicknamed the 'Seep.' In addition, many Jeeps were modified for specific tasks such as transporting stretcher-borne casualties or airborne transportation.

By something of a cruel twist of fate, Bantam lost out. Prototypes for the new army vehicle were prepared by Bantam, Willys-Overland and Ford and much of the original design can be attributed to Karl Probst and Bantam. Ford was responsible for much of the wartime mass production, but it was Willys who produced the penultimate design of the quarter-ton 4x4 and the one that the US Army adopted with a few modifications – the Willys MA, which subsequently became the Willys MB Jeep. Perhaps the highest accolade came from war correspondent Ernie Pyle, later killed by a Japanese sniper's bullet, writing about the North African campaign. "And the Jeep – good Lord, I don't think we could have won the campaign without the Jeep. It did everything, went everywhere, was as faithful as a dog, as strong as mule, and as agile as a goat. It consistently carried twice what it was designed for, and still kept going. I didn't think it even rode so badly after I got used to it. I drove Jeeps thousands of miles, and if I had been called upon to suggest changes from a new model I could have thought of only one or two little things. One was the handbrake.

It was perfectly useless – it wouldn't hold at all. They should have designed one that worked or else saved metal by having none at all. And in the field of acoustics, I wish they could somehow have fixed the Jeep so that at certain speeds the singing of those heavy tires hadn't sounded exactly like an approaching airplane. That little sound effect caused me to jump out of my skin more than once. But except for those two trivial items the Jeep was a divine instrument of wartime locomotion."

Above: *The interior of the MB was distinctly similar in layout to that of the prototype models.*

Below: *The early MBs had a Ford GP-like grille and are now referred to as 'slat grille' MBs.*

Slat Grille Willys MB

Flatfender Jeeps such as this are where all light 4x4s look for their parentage but belong to austere times and show it. Steering locks, key starters and even 12-volt electrics were all in the future when this MB rolled out of the Toledo, Ohio, factory. The body of this mechanical mule was equipped with provision for carrying a shovel, an axe and an aerial. There are numerous detail changes between early MBs such as this and the later ones including the absence of a glove box and 'combat' wheel rims. This example is restored as Jeep of the Headquarters Company of the US 29th Infantry Division.

Specifications

Owner: Unknown
Location: England
Model: Willys MB
Year: 1942
Wheelbase: 80 inches

ENGINE
Model: Flathead four
Capacity: 134.2 cubic inches

TRANSMISSION
Type: Manual 3-speed
Model: Warner T84J
Transfer case: Spicer Model 18

SUSPENSION
Front: Semi-elliptical eight leaf springs
Rear: Semi-elliptical nine leaf springs

AXLES
Front: Fully floating Spicer

Rear: Fully floating Spicer

BRAKES
Front: Drum
Rear: Drum

WHEELS
Type: Steel
Size: 10.5x16 inches

TIRES
Type: Grip tread
Size: 6.00x16 inches

FINISH
Paint: Matt finish
Color: Olive Drab

Above: *Ford built Jeeps to the Willys specification GPWs. This 1944 Jeep, restored by Keith Orpin in England, was one of them supplied under contract (W-20-18-ORD-4920).*

"It is very important that the driver of this vehicle be thoroughly familiar with the various controls and their purpose. The most experienced driver should study the controls because there are a number which are not ordinarily found on standard vehicles."

MAINTENANCE MANUAL FOR WILLYS TRUCK QUARTER-TON 4X4, 1942.

WORLD WAR TWO

FOLLOWING THE JAPANESE attack on Pearl Harbor in December 1941, US soldiers arrived in Britain in January 1942, heralding a new phase in the war that would ultimately lead to the liberation of Europe. The Jeep had arrived before the US Army as lend-lease supplied examples were already in use by the British Army, albeit in limited numbers and in Ford GP and Bantam BRC40 form. The GIs brought more than just Jeeps with them but these novel vehicles soon attracted attention. Norman Longmate recorded this in *The GIs – The Americans in Britain 1942–1945.* "Of all the thousands of American vehicles filling the almost hitherto empty roads of Britain the type which first fascinated and then captivated the civilian population was the Jeep. One Birkenhead man can vividly remember the amazement with which the first Jeep ever to arrive through the Mersey Tunnel was greeted: somewhere around January or February 1942 two strange vehicles came out of the mouth of the almost deserted tunnel. Used as we were to graceful, coach-built cars, the sight of these ungainly, strictly utilitarian vehicles, hung about with shovels, spares and petrol cans caused many heads to turn." Whether it was actually the first Jeep to pass through the toll tunnel under the River Mersey between the ports of

Liverpool and Birkenhead is probably doubtful but it is true that the Jeep bore little resemblance to other comparatively-sized cars of the time. "One British teenager's chief impression of the Jeep was of the gaily painted ridiculous names it so often bore such as The Flying Banana and The Reckless Virgin," wrote Longmate.

The 'Yanks' were, apart from the fights between black and white GIs (the US Army was segregated until almost the end of World War Two), generally popular with the local populations, which itself led to problems of another sort. Longmate noted this in his book. "The early treatment [centre] was, of course, for VD and the establishment was soon well patronized, for the arrival of Jeeps bearing names like Dagwood, Baby Sugar, Honey Child, Pancake and Breezy, was closely followed by the arrival of train-loads of prostitutes from Belfast."

It was North Africa and the Kasserine Pass where many of the GIs first saw combat, followed closely by the Italian campaign from the landings on Sicily. Here, it is said the Mafia ensured unopposed landings for American units, to the beachheads of Salerno and Anzio followed by the long drag into the mountains. Bill Mauldin, the noted cartoonist, was there with the 45th Infantry Division and noted in *Up Front* that even Jeeps had limits. "When the mountain fighting in Italy first started to get tough, and it was impossible for trucks or Jeeps to bring food, water, and ammo up the mountain trails. Mule companies were mustered and calls for experienced mule skinners went out through the divisions. Mules were sought out and bought from farmers. They carried supplies to many soldiers who hadn't seen a Jeep for weeks."

By the time World War Two ended Willys would have built 358,489 MB Jeeps and Ford 277,896 of the GPW. The Jeep's versatility was to be a huge help in winning the war in Europe. "Despite its 'blitzkrieg' fame, the Wehrmacht didn't begin to compare, either in quality, or number, with US motorization. The Germans had nothing comparable to the Jeep or the equally wondrous 2.5-ton truck," wrote Col. Robert S. Allen in his account of

Patton's Third US Army. The MB/GPW Jeep in its final form had two differential-equipped axles mounted to the Jeep's channel section steel chassis by semi-elliptic springs. The gearbox featured three forward gears and one reverse, with a high and low ratio selected by means of an additional gear lever. A third lever enabled the selection of either two- or four-wheel drive; the low ratio gears could only be used in four-wheel drive. The basic steel bodytub was bolted to the chassis, the hood was collapsible and the windshield could be folded forwards onto the hood to present a lower silhouette. The interior was extremely basic and contained little more than basic seats with canvas covered cushions to provide seating for four persons; two in the front on individual seats and a rear bench seat. The exterior of the vehicle had brackets to carry an axe

Below: *The Jeep driver stored his rifle in this carbine rack bolted across the windshield frame. The vertical brackets allow the windshield to open when not folded down.*

and spade, a Jerry can and a spare wheel and tire. It was these mass-produced Jeeps that endeared themselves to soldiers, particularly the frontline troops such as infantry units to whom the Jeep was frequently both a means of supply and a lifesaver. Harold P. Leinbaugh and John D. Campbell, writing about K Company going into action in Europe in 1944, noted, "On paper, K Company was identical to every other rifle outfit heading for the front for the first time. The only thing setting us apart was the K 333 stencilled on the bumpers of our two Jeeps and trailers. On our field jackets we wore with honest pride the red and white Railsplitter patch, an ax cleaving a log." The stencilled marking referred to is that of the US Army's standardized vehicle numbering system. The front bumpers of the two Jeeps would have been stencilled 84-333-I K-1 and K-2 respectively as K Company was one of the constituent rifle companies of the 333rd Infantry

Above: *A restored Jeep in a condition more reminiscent of the appearance of World War Two frontline Jeeps. Windshield cover and half doors were common 'extras.'*

Left: *Jeeps were fitted with brackets for spare wheels and a Jerrycan on the rear of the body tub. This is a British pattern Jerrycan.*

Above: Nicknames were commonly given to Jeeps; comic themes and girls' names were among the most popular.

Right: The British and Canadian Armies also made widespread use of the Jeep. This is a restored British example. The plate that reads 'When in doubt brew up' is a reference to the British habit of frequently drinking tea.

Regiment of the 84th Infantry Division, 'The Railsplitters.' The unit went on to win battle honors in the Ardennes and at Hannover and, according to Leinbaugh and Campbell, it didn't take them long to get used to the way the war was being fought in Europe in the autumn and winter of 1944. "The company needed more firepower and more vehicles. A patrol from the weapons platoon stole a big 4.2 mortar and ammunition from a chemical battalion, and another patrol found a ton-and-a-half truck that belonged to division headquarters. The next night we stole the regimental commander's Jeep but had to give it back when rain washed our white-washed K Company insignia off the bumpers. We escaped with a chewing out – no-one in higher headquarters could devise a punishment sufficient to intimidate a rifle company."

The dogfaces in the units were tight. Mauldin recorded that, "Even though, as in the case of the guys alibiing for each other in the case of the smashed Jeep, the officer will be sore as hell; he will have more respect for them if one of them had come to him privately and whispered in his ear, 'Joe did it.'"

In June of 1944 the Allies splashed ashore in Normandy and prepared themselves to fight all the way to Berlin. The weather worsened as winter tightened its

grip on Europe in 1944, but as always the Willys Jeep delivered the goods. References to its ability in the mud on unsurfaced routes abound in accounts of combat and Bill Mauldin recounted one such tale. "Two hundred miles is a long way for a Jeep, even such a Jeep as my pampered and well-manicured 'Jeanie,' who had covered more than ten thousand miles of Anzio, Italy and France. The ordnance people called her the most neurotic Jeep in Europe. But they cleaned out the carbon, ground the valves and adjusted the carburettor. In spite of all this tender care, Jeanie developed ignition trouble on the way north and I had to stop every few miles in pouring rain and get out and under. After the first one hundred miles I was glad the mud had obliterated the name 'Jeanie' on the Jeep's sides because I was swearing at the car in a way that would have crisped her namesake's lovely ears." The arrival of one particular Jeep signified the start of the Battle of the Hurtgen Forest according to Charles Whiting in the book of the same name. "A Jeep came bumping, bouncing and skidding down the rutted trail carrying a staff messenger for the forward battalion com-

manders. In spite of the morning cold the young men in the holes tensely gripping their weapons started to grow sticky and wet with sweat." The 28th Keystone Infantry Division attempted to wrest Hurtgen Forest – referred to as the 'death factory' by GIs – from the Germans. Whiting went on to describe the Kall Trail, one of the few, barely passable routes into the forest and being used by the Americans as the Main Supply Route (MSR). "A lone Jeep churning its way through the mud, past the wrecked tanks, ran straight into a German patrol. They came slipping out of the trees like gray wolves and opened fire. Tracer zipped lethally through the darkness. The officer in charge screamed, 'Shoot, man! Shoot!' 'I can't Lieutenant,' his driver cried back. 'I'm dying right here!'"

Both the appalling conditions in the forest and the Jeep's abilities are confirmed by Cecil B. Currey. "Four-wheel drive gearboxes chattered as wheels sank hub deep in mud, slewing Carryall trucks and Jeeps erratically along roadways." He went on to describe the Kall trail partially blocked by a disabled American tank. "It

Left: *With the desert war won the British Special Air Service, with their modified and heavily armed Jeeps, were transferred to Europe in 1944. This is a restored example of such a Jeep.*

Right: *To increase the carrying capacity of Jeeps many were field-fitted with a rear basket as seen on this restored Jeep with Canadian unit markings.*

encroached so far onto the narrow trail that even medical Jeeps climbing the hill, grinding up in 'grandma' or super low gear as they came north, were often unable to make it past on the first try." Writing in *Follow Me and Die* of the confusion on the Kall Trail, he went on to say, "All the way down to the river, the convoy repeatedly found it necessary to squeeze against the right bank to allow medical Jeeps carrying wounded to get past them on the way to the rear."

During the fighting around Bastogne in Belgium in December 1944, in what is now known as the Battle of the Bulge, Leinbaugh and Campbell recorded in *The Men of Company K* that Latherial Barnes had a rough week. "'It was tough to get food and ammo up to the men and to keep the Jeep running. The antifreeze had the consistency of sherbet.' Barnes left the kitchen area about four o'clock each morning with breakfast. 'It got awfully cold driving through those hills; it was worse than walking. You couldn't drive along and keep a cigarette going so I chewed tobacco.' Barnes tried to get as close to the company's position as possible, heading up old logging trails in the dark." It wasn't just the enlisted men who were out in Jeeps, as Col. Robert S. Allen pointed out in *Patton's*

Third US Army. "At all hours of the day and night, Patton tore over the roads in his open Jeep, inspiring, prodding, railing and joking." It was a difficult time for all involved. Leinbaugh and Campbell wrote that, "The Jeep reached the company at first light, but a heavy hallucinatory fog had blanketed the area. Unable to spot a single helmet above the line of foxholes, the CO, too tired to react rationally, was convinced K company had been wiped out to a man."

The weather and the conditions took their toll on GIs in many different ways as James Jones noted. "Back in the outfits, the same old grind went on. Fight and run, run and fight. Walk. Walk, walk, walk. A friend of mine had as his Jeep driver an infantryman who had finally refused to walk any more. He had been court martialled

Below: Yank, *a weekly US Army newspaper was among the first publications to feature the postwar Jeep – the CJ-2 and CJ-2A civilian Jeep.*

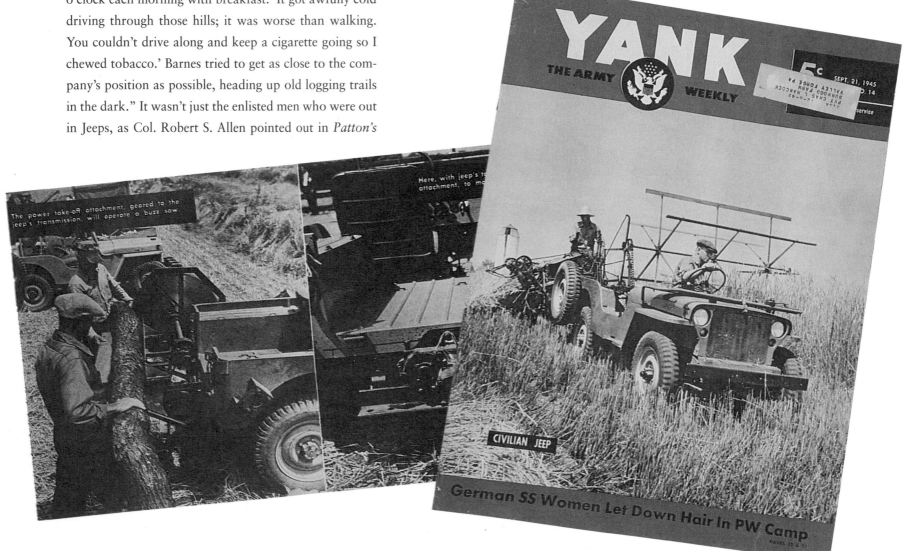

AIRCRAFT DISPERSAL GUIDANCE

69 AV 48   RAF

Above: *Many Jeeps were used by air force and navy units and remained in service after the end of World War Two. This example is restored as a postwar Royal Air Force vehicle.*

for this, given a month in a stockade, and when he came out, had been put to driving my friend's Jeep. This much was okay, drive he would do: walk he wouldn't. He would not even walk to the latrine. When he had to go, he would come out of his shelter, drive the fifty yards to the latrine and hop out. When he had finished his crap, he would drive the Jeep back to the CP. He had made his separate peace." The GI in question wasn't necessarily escaping from all the mundane risks of war such as trench foot because Jeep seats held their own hazards.

During World War Two another of the illnesses that invalided troops was pilonidal sinus, otherwise known as 'Jeep Driver's Ass.' This was a painful abscess that formed in the cleft between the upper buttocks due to the inflammation of a distended hair follicle. There were 77,000 cases of the condition in the US Army alone, mostly caused by the bouncing motion of the Jeep and the insanitary conditions of war.

Death and injury were other risks faced by Jeep drivers in forward areas. Leinbaugh and Campbell recorded

that, "During our weeks on the Rhine, K Company's mess sergeant was the sole casualty. He was wounded by a stray shell while bringing up food in a Jeep. We figured his departure could only improve the quality of our daily meals and Lance's reaction, 'Now there's a German gunner who's really on our side,' was typical." The Germans stretched wires across roads at a height designed to decapitate Jeep drivers and so the anti-decapitation device was developed. It consisted of a vertical bar bolted or welded to the bumper and notched to catch any such wires.

As well as bringing ammunition and food up to the frontline units, Jeeps were regularly used to evacuate casualties. There were specially adapted Jeeps for carrying casualties but, as Leinbaugh and Campbell wrote, it was often the flat hood of the Jeep that had to suffice. "'I

was banged up pretty good,' Gieszl recalls. 'We got Lance on a stretcher on the hood of the Jeep. Max Sobel had been slightly wounded; he and another man helped the two of us back.'" Many a GI had reason to be grateful to the medics, and the Jeep. Mauldin recalls, "It was Charley company with a casualty. The medic took his blankets off the litter he had intended to sleep on, and he carried it out to the medical Jeep, which sat in a revetment of sandbags at the side of the building... They were back in five minutes, because it was only a thousand yards, and they used the Jeep because the hill was steep and the machine was faster than men on foot with a litter. The Germans would have killed the medics just as quickly on foot as with the Jeep, if they had felt like killing medics that night."

Above: *The United States Navy, often nicknamed Uncle Sam's Canoe Club, used Jeeps for a variety of duties as this restored Jeep and trailer suggests.*

Coverage of Jeeps in action during World War Two is not complete without mention of some British organizations that not only pushed the limits of what Jeeps could do, but pioneered much that the automobile itself could do; inadvertently, they developed the concept of 'Jeeping.' Within the rigid structure of the British Army in North Africa existed at least three irregular units, namely the Long Range Desert Group (LRDG), the Special Air Service (SAS) and Popski's Private Army (PPA). These units would raid installations behind enemy lines and were formed by a group of men who had spent the prewar years motoring in the desert for recreation

Left: *Radio Jeeps were fitted with this insulated and spring-mounted MP48 radio aerial base.*

Below: *Dave Goodwin restored this 1943 Willys MB Jeep as a USN Shore Patrol vehicle.*

while working in Egypt. This group, including Ralph Bagnold, Prendergast, Kennedy Shaw and Vladimir Peniakoff (Popski), developed the sand ladder and the sun compass and when war broke out they used their knowledge to help defeat the Germans. The units soon gained a reputation for their audacity in traveling across uncharted desert to raid German airfields and installations. Detailed accounts of their exploits exist in which references to Jeeps abound. Virginia Cowles wrote of the SAS in *The Phantom Major*, "Once in the Wadi they found themselves on a surface made up almost entirely of boulders. Several of the vehicles had their axles broken and it was not uncommon to get two or three punctures within a few minutes. So many Jeeps were crippled that three had to be dismantled for spare parts." Popski

Left: The photos in Yank *magazine show the Civilian Jeep (CJ) being put to a variety of farming tasks including towing a disc harrow.*

remembers desert Jeeping in his book, *Private Army*. "Examining the track step by step on our way back, we came to the conclusion that if we shoved stones, rolled boulders and blasted the rock, we could, with much work, make a very rough track for our Jeeps."

Left: *The later MB Jeep bodies (1943–45 models) incorporated a glove box into the dashboard, seen here with the data plates on. The gearbox cover plate on this Jeep has been temporarily removed for servicing.*

Right: *Power for the Willys MB came from a side-valve in-line four cylinder 60 bhp engine of 134.2 cubic inches displacement.*

Left: *A restored Ford GPA amphibious Jeep belonging to Patrick Kear. The GPA was based on mechanical components from the Ford GPW version of the Jeep as well as a number of specially designed parts.*

Below: *The boat-shaped hull of the GPA was designed by Sparkman and Stephens, a firm of naval architects.*

Amphibious Jeeps were something else altogether. In April 1941 the US National Defense Research Committee (NDRC) had begun work on a quarter-ton amphibian, under the project designation of QMC-4 Truck Light, amphibian. The work was undertaken by Marmon Herrington with the assistance of a firm of naval architects, Sparkman and Stephens Inc and the Ford Motor Company. Design work on the hull shape led to tank tests being run at the Stephens Institute in Hoboken, New Jersey. By this stage the powertrain of the vehicle was Jeep while the frame, hull and fittings were unique to this project vehicle. Work progressed quickly and on February 18 1942 the NDRC was able to demonstrate a fully functional amphibious Jeep on the Huron River in Dearborn, Michigan. At the demonstration were a number of high ranking army personnel who were sufficiently impressed by the amphibian to place orders. Later, surf tests were carried out on a beach near Fort Storey in Virginia. Ford sought contracts to produce large numbers of the Jeep and subsequently obtained them. Between 1942 and 1943 Ford made 12,778 amphibians, designated the GPA. They were based on Ford Jeep (GPW) parts and the A suffix was for amphibious.

The overall concept of the GPA was sound but the cumulative effect of a number of small design faults

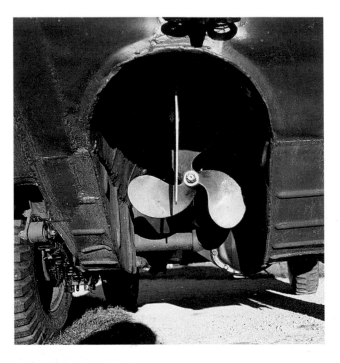

detracted from the overall performance of the vehicle. In military parlance the vehicle was known as the Truck, Amphibian, quarter-ton, 4x4, but it soon became generally referred to as the Seep – a contraction perhaps of sea-Jeep with the obvious reference to water ingress! Used as they were to designing the graceful hulls of yachts, it is unlikely that Sparkman and Stephens had ever designed anything so utilitarian as the GPA, but their hull design ensured that the Seep made ten knots in the water. The propeller was mounted aft in the manner of power boats and the rudder turned in its wake; in the case of the GPA the rudder was turned by the steering wheel. A capstan winch was located on the foredeck, as was a hinged surf shield. The GPA was designed for five people including a crew of two and the seat cushions doubled as life jackets (life preservers). The dash-mounted instruction plates in

Above, left: *The GPA was driven in water by this propeller and steered with a rudder.*

Left: *Drive to the propeller can be engaged/disengaged by means of an additional gear lever and a power take off from the gearbox.*

Above: *For several reasons the GPA was not as successful as it might have been, but in postwar years at least two major expeditions used GPAs.*

the GPA included one that advised on the operation of both the propeller and the bilge pump. According to *Popular Science* magazine of June 1943, 'This seagoing Jeep operates on either land or water, and can pass from one medium to the other with a single minor adjustment by the driver, during which the car doesn't have to stop.' The 'single minor adjustment' was, of course, engaging the drive to the propeller. Writing in *Half Safe*, Ben Carlin, who crossed the Atlantic Ocean in a GPA, summed up the amphibious Jeep thus: "The [amphibi-

ous] Jeep was useless in ship to shore lighterage, the forte of its big brother DUKW which could carry two and a half tons anywhere. Nor could it compete with collapsible boats at ferrying troops across rivers. Its military uses were pretty well confined to light amphibious reconnaissance, ferrying high-powered generals, and serving as bait for nurses and Red Cross girls. All in all amphibious jeeping was an extremely sporting pastime pursued with rather more élan than success by run of the mill service drivers from Wichita and Hogsnorton-on-the-hill."

US Navy Shore Patrol Jeep

By the time this Willys MB Jeep was made in 1943, both Ford and Willys were building Jeeps in vast numbers with only minor differences between the two designs. Jeep production for each company was further divided into early, standard and composite models which again varied only in details. Jeeps were used in both the European Theater of Operations (ETO) and the Pacific Theater of Operations (PTO) by servicemen from all the Allied nations. This model was supplied to Norway in the postwar years before being acquired by Dave Goodwin in England, who restored it as a US Navy Shore Patrol Jeep.

Specifications

Owner: Dave Goodwin
Location: Doncaster, England
Model: Willys MB
Year: 1943
Wheelbase: 80 inches

ENGINE
Model: Flathead four
Capacity: 134.2 cubic inches

TRANSMISSION
Type: Manual 3-speed
Model: T84J
Transfer case: Spicer Model 18

SUSPENSION
Front: Semi-elliptical eight leaf springs
Rear: Semi-elliptical nine leaf springs

AXLES
Front: Fully floating Spicer
Rear: Fully floating Spicer

BRAKES
Front: 9-inch drum
Rear: 9-inch drum

WHEELS
Type: Kelsey Hayes Combat
Size: 4.50x16 inches

TIRES
Type: Grip tread
Size: 6.00x16 inches

FINISH
Paint: United States Navy
Color: Gray

Above: *The CJ-2A was introduced in 1946. Its resemblance to the Willys MB is obvious although the headlamps are bigger and the maker's name is in evidence.*

"A Jeep now and again travels up Yankee Hill to the old site of Yankee. A few cabins and mine holes remain as souvenirs of past activity here."

GUIDE TO THE COLORADO GHOST TOWNS AND MINING CAMPS.
PERRY EBERHART. 1959.

THE POSTWAR YEARS

THE HISTORY OF the various vehicles to have carried the Jeep name is considerably shorter than many of the other American manufacturers. The reason for this is that although Jeep is both a model-type and a brandname, it has been owned by a variety of manufacturers and the Jeep vehicle itself originated out of the Quarter-Ton 4x4 reconnaissance truck of the US Army. In many ways, the various immediate postwar Jeeps pioneered the contemporary mass market for four-wheel drive vehicles.

Even before the end of World War Two, Willys-Overland of Toledo, Ohio, knew it was onto a good thing with the Jeep – its product and its trademark – that had served the Allied military so well in every theater of operations. Willys-Overland had the foresight to register Jeep as its own trademark and began to prepare for the production of civilian Jeeps which were to be designated as CJs. Willys knew that a civilian Jeep would be a versatile machine for all sorts of agricultural and commercial tasks. As early as 1942 the Department of Agriculture (DOA) investigated the agricultural possibilities of the Jeep. Two military Jeeps, a used GPW and a new MB, were tested during April of that year at the DOA's Farm Tillage Machinery Laboratory in Auburn, Alabama. The Jeeps were evaluated in use with plows and harrows. The DOA felt that the Jeep was too narrow, too low, that it was geared too high for field use and needed a drawbar and lift for attaching implements. However, they did feel that when fitted with a PTO the Jeep was a good vehicle for running pumps, conveyors and other machinery. Willys-Overland was not enamored at the prospect of war-surplus Jeeps being distributed at knock-down prices to farmers because it saw a future in specific civilian models. George Ritter, Vice President at Willys, prepared a report about the proposed civilian Jeeps. The specification included a rear PTO, lower ratio transmission, drawbar hitch, larger diameter clutch and stronger chassis. It is believed that the first civilian Jeep prototype was constructed and ready for evaluation by May 1944. It was designated the CJ-1 AgriJeep. The CJ-1 was a modified Willys MB, while the CJ-2 was built from the ground up from components specified by the manufacturer including axles from Spicer and a body from American Central. Various types of CJ-2s were made including a batch described as AgriJeeps. The total production of CJ-1 and CJ-2 models numbered less than 50 and it was the CJ-2A that would become the first mass-produced civilian model.

The CJ-2A featured the same four cylinder L-head Go-Devil engine and 80-inch wheelbase as the MB but included a revised transmission and axles. Differential and transmission ratios were also changed. More obvious alterations included the inclusion of a hinged tailgate to facilitate easier loading and relocation of the spare wheel to the vehicle's side. There were also numerous detail improvements including bigger headlights – made possible by reducing the number of pressed apertures in the grille from nine to seven – and a relocated gas cap as well as the maker's name pressed into several of the panels. The civilian models were offered in a variety of colors to make them more appealing to the civilian market. Initially the Jeep CJs were marketed for agricultural purposes by dint of their being equipped with power take offs (it was possible to specify either front, rear or centre power take off as an extra cost option) and agricultural drawbars. They were promoted through being used in a variety of farming tasks such as towing plows and disc harrows. Other early variants included Jeeps fitted with fire fighting equipment made by The Howe Fire Apparatus Co of Anderson, Indiana.

Production of the CJ-2A lasted until 1949, by which time 214,202 had been produced. This produc-

Above: *The CJ-2A featured the same arrangement of instruments as the Willys MB,* with a speedometer, fuel gauge, oil pressure gauge, ammeter and water temperature gauge

Right: *Over the years many flatfender Jeeps have been modified for recreational use. This one has a rollbar, bikini top, bullbar and oversize wheels and tires.*

tion run overlapped with the second of the CJs – the CJ-3A. This Jeep went into mass production in 1948 and was built until 1953. The main differences between the CJ-2A and CJ-3A were a further strengthened transmission and transfer case and a one-piece windshield. In 1953 the CJ-3B was introduced with a noticeably different silhouette because of a higher hood line. This change was necessary in order to permit Willys to fit a new engine. The Hurricane F-head four cylinder was a taller engine that displaced the same 134 cubic inches but produced more horsepower. The CJ-3B would stay in production until the sixties and a total of 155,494 were constructed. This model CJ would live on until the present day through a series of licensing agreements that meant it would be produced in a variety of European, Indian and Japanese factories by manufacturers such as Hotchkiss, Mahindra and Mitsubishi respectively. Kaiser-Frazer and Willys-Overland merged in 1953 and the resulting Jeep-building company became known as Kaiser Jeep.

Discussion of postwar Jeep products would be incomplete without mention of the various station wagons produced by the companies who owned the Jeep trademark over the years. Production of the Jeep Station Wagon – America's first all-steel station wagon – started in 1946. It was essentially a traditionally styled station wagon, with pressed steel sides but with a Jeep-type grille and hood with chrome details. The body was mounted on a steel chassis which was fitted with Jeep's proven engine and running gear. Through the years different paint schemes, details, trim levels and advertising ploys were used, all of which ensured that the Station Wagon stayed in production until 1962 when it was replaced by the Wagoneer. The Wagoneer was also a 4x4 station wagon but considerably more modern in both styling and engineering.

Willys-Overland had diversified from the production of the basic Jeep into the production of working trucks including the one-ton range of 4x4 models. These were a series of trucks based around the same chassis, mechanical parts and front sheetmetal as the Willys sedan delivery, the 4-75 models. They were available in two- and four-wheel drive variants and

Left: *Barry Redman driving his modified 1947 CJ-2A Jeep.*

Above: *The CJ-2A was frequently modified to enhance its performance. This one is powered by a* *Chevrolet V8 and also has a rollcage, a stainless-steel grille, alloy wheels and freewheeling hubs.*

with different payloads. The designation changed from time to time; by 1957, for example, the one-ton, four cylinder engined 4x4 pickup had been tagged the F4-134. It was still the same general design that Willys-Overland had introduced in the immediate postwar years to capitalize on the success of the Willys Jeep by offering a commercial variant. This was a long wheelbase pickup with a closed cab but frontal styling that resembled the Willys MB. The first of these were offered alongside the station wagons in 1947 and the model survived the 1953 acquisition of Willys-Overland by the Kaiser Manufacturing Company. With various minor upgrades and styling changes it would run through until the sixties. After 1962 the trucks were redesigned with a much more modern appearance but both models were produced in paral-

Above: *Willys-Overland, makers of the CJ-2A pressed their name into several of the Jeep's panels including the hood.*

Left: *Like that of its military predecessors, the windshield of the CJ-2A folds flat onto the hood.*

lel for a few years. Another type of Jeep truck was the forward control type, although it was frequently bodied as a walk-in panel van. The idea behind these machines was that by putting the cab over the front axle and engine it created a larger load bed while still retaining a relatively short wheelbase. The 4x4 Jeep models were first introduced in 1957 and stayed in production for seven years. There were two models, the FC-150 and FC-170. The FC prefix clearly stands for forward control and the numerical designation refers to the wheelbase. The FC-150 was based around the 81-inch wheelbase of the CJ-5 then in production while the FC-170 was based on a 103.5-inch wheelbase chassis. The short wheelbase model had a four cylinder engine and the longer one a six. Other components of the machines were similar – both utilized leaf sprung axles, drum brakes, two-speed transfer boxes and three-speed gearboxes. Yet another commercial Jeep introduced in the late fifties was the CJ-6, a long wheelbase version of the CJ-5 sharing front and rear sheetmetal, axles, engine and transmission, but simply having an extra 20 inches in the wheelbase.

That there was a major shift in society's attitudes and values after the war is well known. One way in which this manifested itself in connection with Jeeps is that the war expanded the horizons of many. Writing in *Hail to the Jeep* – the first book to sing the Jeep's praises – A. Wade Wells noted in 1946 that, "Thanks to the Jeep, travel will no longer be confined to the major highways and traffic arteries; weekend 'Jeeping' can be an adventure along unexplored bypaths and trails." The terminology of Jeeps, Jeeping and Jeepers was becoming established. A humorous note in Elinore Carlin's diary described a slightly dishevelled arrival in Lages des Flores, Azores: "We were the best dressed Jeepers within fifty yards as Half Safe waltzed up the straight." Elinore Carlin's diary was quoted by her husband Ben in *Half Safe*, an account of a trip by

Right: *This CJ-2A features aftermarket parts including a Bestop roof, ACME stainless-steel tailgate and radial tires on alloy wheels.*

Left: *To make the CJ-2A suitable for civilian use it was fitted with a body-side fuel filler-cap and a hinged rear tailgate.*

Right: *The A-frame fitted to the front of this CJ-2A was another military idea that became popular with recreational Jeep users – it meant the Jeep could be towed behind another vehicle such as a camper.*

the couple, who took the concept of Jeeping further than many. Ben Carlin was born in Northam, Western Australia, in 1912 while his wife Elinore was born in Watertown, Massachusetts. They met while serving in India during World War Two, which is also where Ben Carlin first saw a GPA and had the idea of a round-the-world trip in one. He explained his motivation thus: "I have always been interested in salt water, small boats and vehicles and fancy I know something about them all." Ben Carlin planned to buy a surplus amphibian and obtain the backing of the manufacturer for his proposed trip. Inexplicably he went to Willys-Overland in Toledo, Ohio, when in truth the GPA was wholly Ford. Willys-Overland was reportedly less than impressed and even Carlin had doubts. "Had an amphibious Jeep ever crossed a really large body of water – like Lake Erie? No? Then what reason had I to think that I could charm one into doing so? I wasn't even a professional seaman." He went on to say, "Damn it – I would leave the States either in a seagoing amphibious Jeep or via the Dead-beats Department of Ellis Island."

He eventually bought a GPA from the surplus auction at Aberdeen Proving Ground in Baltimore, Maryland – the chances are it was one of the GPAs used to test the design by the US Army. After a period

of preparation and modification the GPA, christened Half Safe, was outward bound in July 1950, with Ben and Elinore aboard. They left Canada for Nova Scotia, The Azores, Madeira, The Canary Islands, West Africa, Gibraltar, Portugal and up through Europe to cross the English Channel to England. The log of the Carlins' transatlantic voyage saw the use of nautical terminology rarely used in conjunction with Jeeps: "We were raring to go when at 7pm the wind was still blowing 25, veered to SSW and we got underway on course 95 degrees. The confused sea on the beam slowed the Jeep." Though Carlin's book *Half Safe* ends in England, Ben Carlin went on to circumnavigate the globe, covering an estimated 9600 nautical miles and 39,000 statute miles overland. The GPA returned to Canada in May 1958 and from here Carlin shipped it home to Australia. The second half of the journey is described in *The Other Half of Half Safe* which was only published after Carlin's death in 1981 and his GPA is preserved at his old school, Guildford Grammar, in Western Australia.

It wasn't only Australians who set out to see far off places by Jeep in the early postwar years. On May 1st 1949 a Belgian, Joe Ceurvorst, left Brussels, Belgium in a war-surplus MB called 'Mosquito' on a 22,000 mile journey. With him went a female relative, Jane Barbier and his dog Pelish. They disembarked from the ferry from Europe in Algiers and headed south across the Sahara Desert by way of Colomb Bechar, Adrar and Reggane. When they reached the Atlantic coast of Dahomey (Benin) they pointed the Jeep eastwards through the Belgian Congo (Zaire), Uganda and Kenya. The route then took the travellers north to Egypt and along the North African coast where the journey reads like a gazetteer of the Desert War; Cairo, Alexandria, El Alamein, Sollum, Tobruk, Tripoli and Tunis. The journey was recounted in *L'Afrique en Jeep* which was later published in English as *Africa in a Jeep*. Of his MB, Ceurvorst wrote, 'Although my particular Jeep lacked comfort, it did possess the necessary qualities to cope with the most difficult terrain.' In the mid-fifties two female

American college professors also disembarked in Algiers and headed south across the Sahara in a Jeep. Dorothy Rogers and Louise Ostberg crossed the desert, drove through the Congo and headed to South Africa. They then drove north to Egypt and headed west along the north African coast in a Willys Station Wagon. The journey totalled 25,000 miles and took the pair six months. On their return to the US, Dorothy Rogers wrote *Jeopardy and a Jeep* which was published in 1957.

As well as being the means of overland travel there was a place in colonial Africa – largely unaffected by World War Two – for the Jeep. In her book of 1957, *I Married a Hunter,* Marjorie Michael wrote that "The dogs were the first to hear George's Jeep coming around the corner of our road, and they dashed off at once almost knocking the children over in their haste to welcome back their master." The book, which contains photographs of a CJ-2A on V-rib implement tires and a Willys Station Wagon, records the minutiae of African life and trips into the Kalahari desert as well as the altogether more exciting business of diamond smuggling! The diamonds were disguised as packets of Jeep spares, about which she says, "He [Jarvis] had time to consider the serious defect in his timing which allowed him to have a box of diamonds in the toolbox of his Jeep at a time when a CID decided to search it."

South America was another continent still to be explored by Jeep in the early postwar years. In 1947 two Frenchmen, Daniel Barby and Henri Boucher, left New York in a brand new CJ-2A and travelled south through Mexico, Guatemala, El Salvador, Honduras, Nicaragua, Peru, Chile, Argentina and reached Patagonia. The account of their travels was a French-language book, *New York Patagonie ou 35000 Kilometres en Jeep,* published in 1950. Another notable journey in South America involved a married couple and a GPA. Frank and Helen Schreider met as students in postwar California. Frank was a WWII USN submarine veteran. The couple swapped their car for a used Jeep and made plans to travel to South

Left: *The CJ-3A was the next civilian Jeep and went into production in late 1948. This example has been modified for recreational fourwheeling in Colorado. It is fitted with Rancho shock absorbers, alloy wheels, Goodrich tires, a winch and high-back seats.*

America on a belated honeymoon. In order to prepare for the journey they bought war-surplus camping equipment, learned Spanish and learned to drive off-road. This latter preparation was done in the excavations for the building of the Medical School at the UCLA University where gradients and sideslopes abounded! The Schreiders left California in February 1951 and over the next four months drove 6,000 miles across six countries. They sold the Jeep in San José, Costa Rica, for the price of their passage home. The Jeeping bug had bitten hard so the couple began the search for a serviceable GPA.

A Los Angeles company had bought a number of war-surplus GPAs for use as ice cream wagons but they were beyond economic repair to be seaworthy again. Eventually Frank Schreider found one and began to prepare it for a journey. The preparation took three years and a period of work in Alaska which led to the plan – to drive from Circle, Alaska, to Ushuaia, Tierra Del Fuego – becoming a reality. On June 21 1954 the couple and their dog Dinah drove south from Alaska to where their GPA was in storage and finished their preparations. The GPA was completed with a cabin so that it could double as transport and accommodation and christened La Tortuga. As well as driving, winching and swimming their way south, the Schreiders achieved a Jeeping first; the first commercial transit of an amphibian through the Panama Canal. The overall journey covered more than 22,000 miles and was documented in the couple's book of the journey, *La Tortuga. An Amphibious Journey from Alaska to Tierra Del Fuego*. Much of the narrative is concerned with the maintenance of the GPA and the improvization needed to keep it rolling and swimming despite a shortage of spares. Frank Schreider recalled an enforced service halt in Colombia. "I sat in the Jeep staring through the hole in the floorboards at the black oily interior of the transmission. If only the engineers who had designed these things, I thought, had tried to work on them. If only the synchronizers could be kept closer together, then they couldn't slip out of alignment. A spacer

Far left: *In the postwar years Willys-Overland capitalized on the success of the wartime Jeep by offering a range of four-wheel drive pickups and station wagons alongside the civilian Jeeps. This is a 1957 four-wheel drive version of the pickup.*

Right: *The interior of the Jeep trucks was basic but functional; three gear levers enabled selection of gears, four-wheel drive and low range. The Willys-Overland logo adorns the horn push in the steering wheel.*

Far right: *The Jeep-like grille of the trucks was dressed up with chrome trims later in the production run which lasted from 1947 to 1965.*

behind them would do it – if only I had a spacer. But even if I did I would still have to pull the transmission to install it. But a split spacer might be the answer – if I had one. What a lot of wishful 'ifs.' Then I had an idea. That old standby, baling wire. If it worked we might be able to make it to Bogota."

Jeeping closer to home was also becoming popular. In 1952 a group of Rotarians met in Georgetown, California, to discuss ways of boosting the economy of their Norcal town. They decided on hosting an annual Jeep run across the Sierra Nevada mountains on the Rubicon Trail. The event – the Jeepers Jamboree – was

first run in 1953 and attracted 155 people in 55 Jeeps. Jeepers Jamborees still cross the Rubicon Trail which runs from Georgetown to Lake Tahoe over obstacles with names like The Big Sluice, Granite Slab and Walker's Rock. The Jeepers Jamboree is now one of an annual series of Jeep-sponsored Jeep Jamborees held around the United States including the Ouray, Colorado Jeep Jamboree. The State of Colorado was another place where Jeeps soon found a place amongst recreationalists. The state with many miles of ruinous mining trails in its mountains saw the Mile-Hi Jeep Club founded in 1956. Kurland Motors, a Jeep deal-

ership, sent out letters to Jeep owners and at a meeting in August 1956 the showroom was packed with approximately 500 Jeepers who formed the first four-wheel drive club in Colorado. The club was chartered by the state in July 1957 and a red, white and blue logo of a Jeep climbing Mount Elbert was adopted. The club thrives to this day.

The Korean War started on June 25 1950 when North Korean soldiers invaded South Korea by crossing the 38th Parallel, the line at which the country had been arbitrarily partitioned in 1945. In response to the outbreak of this war the US Department of Defense reactivated the Ordnance Tank Automotive Center in Detroit, Michigan in order to again mobilize the US auto industry for war production. The United Nations committed troops to aid South Korea and the Jeep was among their equipment. For the GIs on the frontline it was just as dangerous as the fighting on Tarawa or in the Ardennes and the same dangers and hardships lurked around each corner. "As the Jeep stopped [Captain Jack] Bolt looked across the paddy in the bright moonlight and saw a group of men approaching the road. He thought they were retreating Americans until they reached a point about fifty yards from the road and opened fire. Bolt shouted to his dri-

ver to get out of there, and they sped down the road." So wrote Edwin P. Hoyt in *The Bloody Road to Panmunjon*. If it wasn't communist soldiers it was land mines or the weather. "Either the Chinese had laid mines along the road during the winter or they had done it since. The patrol made it through safely, but later in the day when the road had thawed in the sun, a Jeep was blown up by a landmine." The Korean

War continued into 1951 as the People's Republic of China sent troops and assistance to the communist North Koreans. In order to avoid raising the stakes too high, President Truman was forced to sack General MacArthur, the UN Commander in Chief when he talked of invading China. This UN 'Police Action' led to restrictions on the amount of certain metals – including zinc, chromium, tin and nickel –

Below: A 1961 Willys 6-75 4x4 Station Wagon. Two-tone paint was a factory option.

Right: *Production of Willys
Station Wagons ran from
1946 to 1965 and they
were offered in both
standard and deluxe forms.
This is the brochure for the
deluxe model.*

Right: *Production of Willys
Station Wagons ran from
1946 to 1965 and they
were offered in both
standard and deluxe forms.
This is the brochure for the
deluxe model.*

that could be used by the American auto industry for
work other than that related to defence. Numerous
other restrictions came into force as a result of this latest conflict, the National Production Agency (NPA)
limiting both car and truck production in order to
ensure a continuous flow of equipment for the war.
Much of the equipment used in Korea was of WWII
vintage, including Jeeps, but a new model did appear
in 1950. It was the M38 (sometimes known as the
MC) and was essentially a CJ-3A designed for military
use. The upgrades included a semi-floating rear axle,
24-volt electrical system and military lights. A total of
60,345 were made of which a percentage saw service
in Korea. The Korean War dragged on through 1952,
the year that Republican Dwight D. Eisenhower was
elected president, and ended only after the agreement
at Panmunjon in July 1953. The cost had been high,
including 51,000 American deaths, and the face of
world politics had now changed beyond recognition.
The Korean War was the first confrontation of the big

powers in the nuclear age and set the stage for the
brinkmanship of numerous cold war-era conflicts to
come.

Another Jeep was built specifically for the military
– the M38A1 (also known as the MD) – from 1951
onward. It was slightly larger than the 'flatfenders'

that had come before it as its wheelbase was one inch longer, but as the nickname of the early models perhaps indicates, its fenders were not flat. The hood and fenders were curved, although the vehicle was still basic and featured a flat-sided design and a grille that was recognizably a Jeep. The M38A1 was powered by the F-head Hurricane engine as fitted to the CJ-3B. A civilian version of the M38A1 was introduced during 1955 and designated the CJ-5. The CJ-6 was another model that appeared at the same time. It was simply a longer version of the CJ-5 aimed at giving commercial users a much larger load area, with a 101-inch wheelbase compared to the 81-inch wheelbase of the CJ-5. These various designations skip that of the CJ-4 and it is believed that only one prototype had this designation. One possible reason that it was not developed is because of the restrictions on the required materials imposed as a result of the Korean War. The CJ-5 was justly to become the most famous of all the civilian Jeeps.

Willys 4x4 Pickup

*The 1957 one-ton four cylinder engined F4-134 4x4
Pickup was of the general designs that Willys-Overland
introduced in the immediate postwar years to capitalize on
the success of the Willys Jeep. This was a longer wheelbase
pickup with a closed cab but frontal styling that resembled
the Willys Jeep. First offered in 1947, the model survived
the acquisition of Willys-Overland by Kaiser and, with
minor upgrades and styling changes, would run until the
sixties. After 1962 the trucks were redesigned with a much
more modern appearance. Barry Redman restored this
truck using parts from several trucks and three countries.*

Specifications

Owner: Barry Redman
Location: Reading,
England
Model: F4-134 Pickup
Year: 1957
Wheelbase: 118 inches

ENGINE
Model: Hurricane I-4
Capacity: 134.2 cubic
inches

TRANSMISSION
Type: Manual
Model: Warner 3-speed
Transfer case: Spicer
Model 18

SUSPENSION
Front: Semi-elliptical
nine leaf springs
Rear: Semi-elliptical 11
leaf springs

AXLES
Front: Fully floating
Spicer Model 23
Rear: Semi-floating
Timken 51340

BRAKES
Front: 11 inch drums
Rear: 11 inch drums

WHEELS
Type: Steel
Size: 5x16 inches

TIRES
Type: Grip tread
Size: 7.00x16 inches

FINISH
Paint: Owner
Color: President Red

Above: *The US Army's M38 Jeep had largely been superseded by the M38A1 and MUTT 4x4s by the time of the Vietnam War but its military use continued in numerous other countries.*

"My visit to the town of Danang itself left me with many impressions. Streets crammed with Jeeps, six-bys, troop carriers and a madhouse of cycles. Hordes of people carrying great baskets on opposite ends of a pole across their shoulders."

AIR WAR – VIETNAM. FRANK HARVEY. 1967.

THE VIETNAM WAR

ON NOVEMBER 9 1960, the Democrat John F. Kennedy was elected US President. The sixties was to be a troubled decade for the American nation; on December 22 1961, James Davis from Tennessee became the first American serviceman killed in Vietnam. Less than a month later, on January 12 1962, Operation Ranch Hand took place to defoliate parts of Vietnam using the chemical Agent Orange. The Bay of Pigs fiasco and the Cuban Missile Crisis followed as cold war tensions heightened. In August 1963 Martin Luther King made his historic speech at the Lincoln Memorial in Washington DC and in November President Kennedy was assassinated in Dallas, Texas. Lyndon Baines Johnson, the Vice-President who was with Kennedy on the trip to Texas, was sworn in as the 35th US President. The US commitment to South Vietnam would grow quickly; in March 1965 two battalion landing teams of the US Marine Corps were the first ground combat troops committed to Vietnam and on December 3 1965 LBJ compared Vietnam to the Alamo. In 1966 the Vietnam War cost America $5.8 billion.

The war in Vietnam continued and in 1967 the US Army was consuming 850,000 tons of supplies and 80 million gallons of gasoline monthly. At the end of January 1968 the Viet Cong launched the Tet Offensive against Saigon, Hue and other South Vietnamese cities and places such as Khe Sanh and Da Nang became committed to the pages of history books. In 1969 the USA spent $28.8 billion fighting the Vietnam War. Even though the war became noted as the first 'helicopter war,' with the Bell HU-1 'Huey' synonymous with images of Vietnam, the US Army needed wheeled vehicles. Updated versions of the deuce-and-a-half and the Jeep were used. Robert Mason was a helicopter pilot in Vietnam between 1965 and 1966, and in his book *Chickenhawk* he wrote, "I flared steeply at 200 feet to slow the Huey for the landing. Just above the top of my instrument panel, at the south end of the Golf Course, I saw a man waving his arms as he stood on a Jeep." Jeeps were used to marshal the helicopters as they flew in and were waiting when the dust-off choppers landed. "A Jeep drove him and the other pilot across the airstrip to the hospital tent." In *The Siege of Khe Sahn: An Oral History*, Eric Hammel quotes 1st Lt Paul Elkan, Bravo Battery, 13th Marine Regiment: "'We medevacked Private Smart in a Jeep. His back looked like he had been whipped with a cat-o'-nine tails. It was shredded. He was shaking so hard from shock and the cold that the Jeep shook.'"

Examination of photos taken during the Vietnam War reveals that at least four types of Jeep were used by the US and South Vietnamese forces. These included the M38A1 and M170 models, short and long wheelbase Jeeps respectively, with the M170 used as an ambulance. Also used was the M606, the military version of the CJ-3B and the military version of the licence-built CJ-3B, the Mitsubishi J4. Two other light 4x4 vehicles were used in Vietnam by the US Army – the Ford M151A MUTT and the American Motors M422 Mighty Mite. Some would say that these vehicles are not true 'Jeeps,' but they filled the US Army's need for a quarter-ton 4x4 in the Vietnam War era. The M151 was built by Ford after almost a decade of design and testing. It was different from the quarter-ton 4x4s that had preceded it because the body and chassis were integral and the suspension was independent all round through the use of coil springs. The M151 MUTT – Military Utility Tactical Truck – was manufactured by Ford between 1960 and 1962 and by Willys (later Kaiser) from 1962 and 1963. This was followed by a slightly upgraded version, the M151A1, made by Kaiser, then Ford, between 1964 and 1968. There

were also recoilless rifle and ambulance variants – the M151A1C and M718 respectively. These MUTTs had unusual handling characteristics which, reportedly, gave them a propensity to rolling over while in use. As a result, the US Army asked Ford to redesign the vehicle in 1968 to improve the handling while maintaining parts interchangeability with its existing MUTTs. The redesigned vehicles were designated the M151A2 series. A number of detail changes were made to the vehicle but the major change was the redesigning of the rear suspension. Instead of a swinging A-frame design the new models were fitted with a twin trailing arm system which still provided independent rear suspension. The ambulance and recoilless rifle variants were the M718A1 and the M825. Production of the second series lasted from 1969 until 1978 for the US Army but ran into the eighties for export sales.

As Robert Mason recounts, exactly which type of Jeep was which didn't bother many US military personnel at times. "Somehow we missed the truck back to camp.

Right: The M38A1 model was modified for use with recoilless rifles and became known as the M38A1C. These were also used by various NATO Armies including Dutch-built NEKAF examples.

Left: Despite its more curved fenders, the M38A1 still resembled the earlier Jeeps in its layout. The fuel tank remained under the seat, transmission layout was the same, and the seats and dashboard layout were similar.

Left: *The M38A1 was a true military vehicle in the way that earlier Jeeps had been. This included being fitted with a machine gun mount and radio equipment. This restored Vietnam War-era Jeep has both.*

Below: *The military specification M38A1 Jeep became the basis of the civilian CJ-5, although its interior and fittings were considerably refined in the process.*

We went back to the Officers' Club and borrowed one of their Jeeps. We didn't tell them we were borrowing it; it was made in America after all. When the Jeep was found the next day parked in the Camp Holloway motor pool, it caused a stink." Indeed, it is difficult to find the quarter-ton 4x4s referred to as anything other than 'jeeps' in almost all Vietnam veterans' accounts of the war. The vehicles were marked in a manner not dissimilar to that used in WWII. In *Tank Sergeant*, Ralph Zumbro described his arrival by helicopter at 69th Armor in Vietnam in 1967: "I helped them offload, and they lifted out, leaving me standing alone and somewhat bemused on an empty helipad. A Jeep drove up and, with some relief, I saw A-1/69 on its bumper." This signified that the Jeep was from A Company, the 1st Battalion, in 69th Armor Division.

During February and March 1968 the US Army withstood a siege of one of its positions south of the 17th Parallel near the border with Laos. The place was the Khe Sanh Combat Base (KSCB) garrisoned by the US Marine Corps. It was encircled and the resupply came from the air. The supply planes always brought NVA fire down on the base. Eric Hammel documented the ordeal in *The*

Left: *MUTTs (Military Utility Tactical Trucks) were made by Willys, Ford and Kaiser to fulfil the US Army's need for a quarter-ton 4x4 in the Vietnam War era. GIs called them 'Jeeps.'*

Below: *The immediate difference between a Jeep and a MUTT is that the MUTT has a horizontally slotted radiator grille.*

Above: *A restored Vietnam War MUTT. The MUTT models were progressively upgraded through their production run.*

Siege of Khe Sahn: An Oral History. Corporal Dennis Smith was with Bravo Company of the 1st Battalion 26th Marines: "'One of the guys in my supply section was L Cpl Virgil Crunk from Ohio. All he wanted to do when he got out was drive a truck and listen to country music. He had an uncanny way of finding anything he needed on that base. If he couldn't make a trade or a deal for something he stole it. I never asked where things came from. He ordered his parts for his Jeep direct from Motor Transport and used their tools to maintain it. He was the fastest Jeep at Khe Sahn, proven over and over on the airstrip against other drivers.' Smith went on, 'As soon as the cargo skid was pulled from a plane, Virgil was out on the runway, throwing anything and everything into his Jeep trailer. Then he was out of there in the fastest Jeep at Khe Sanh. Once, as rockets were slamming into the base, I watched him take a curve into our area so fast that the trailer flipped over. He dragged it in upside down and jumped into the hooch – laughing. Virgil was kind of hard on Jeep trailers.'"

The last year of the sixties was the year that two Americans, Neil Armstrong and Buzz Aldrin, became the first men to land on the moon as the United States won the space race. Overshadowing this, though, was some-

thing else that the US seemingly could not win – the Vietnam War. In May 1969 units of the US Army and South Vietnamese forces attempted to take Hill 937 – Hamburger Hill – in the A Shua Valley east of the Laotian border. It turned into one of the bloodiest battles of the Vietnam War and provoked heavy criticism in the US as the hill had little strategic value. On September 5 1970 Operation Jefferson Glenn began. It was carried out by troops of the 101st Airborne Division (Airmobile) and infantry units of the South Vietnamese Army against Charlie in Vietnam's Thua Thien Province. The operation was to be the last major military operation in Vietnam in which US ground troops would participate. Faced with ever increasing opposition to the war, the seventies would see President Richard M. Nixon scaling down and subsequently ending US involvement in the Vietnam War. On January 27 1973 the signing of the Peace Accords in Paris, France, brought to an end the Vietnam War. It had been the longest war in American history and the nation had suffered in excess of 58,000 killed or missing in action. The war had significant socio-economic effects on the nation which included the resignation of a president, the political turmoil it engendered and the economic problems of the early seventies.

Kaiser Jeep M38A1

This is a restored example of the M38A1 Jeep, manufactured by the Kaiser Jeep Corporation to fulfil military contracts. They were also built in other countries including Holland and Canada. There were numerous specialist variants of the M38A1 including the M38A1C, the M38A1D, the M606A2, the M606A3 and the M170. Similar variants of the MUTT were later built. Of the new M38A1, Devon Francis writing in the Standard Fact Book of Cars for 1953 *said, "Whatever designation it bears, it will still be a half pint truck in olive drab. You didn't join the Army to ride around in Rolls-Royces, soldier."*

Specifications

Owner: Unknown
Location: England
Model: M38A1
Year: 1965
Wheelbase: 81 inches

ENGINE
Model: F-head four
Capacity: 134.2 cubic inches

TRANSMISSION
Type: Manual 3-speed
Model: Warner T090A
Transfer case: Spicer Model 18

SUSPENSION
Front: Semi-elliptical 12 leaf springs
Rear: Semi-elliptical 13 leaf springs

AXLES
Front: Fully floating Spicer 25
Rear: Semi-floating Spicer 44-2

BRAKES
Front: 9-inch drums
Rear: 9-inch drums

WHEELS
Type: Kelsey-Hayes steel disc
Size: 4.50x16 inches

TIRES
Type: Michelin XCL
Size: 7.00x16 inches

FINISH
Paint: Matt finish
Color: Olive Drab

Above: *Jim's CJ is a massively modified CJ-7 built for recreational fourwheeling and seen here on the slickrock of Moab, Utah.*

> *"It is a long tedious drive for the 120-odd miles from Mexicali to San Felipe but the road is paved and, except for a ten-mile stretch which is a little rough, is in good condition. Tired and cold (there was no heater in my Jeep), we stumbled into the modern hotel which had been erected there."*

ERLE STANLEY GARDNER. HUNTING THE DESERT WHALE. 1961.

CHANGING TIMES

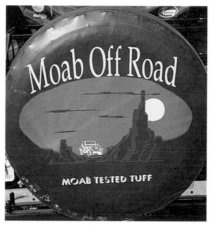

JIM CULLEN PONDERED on the place of the automobile in American society: "Ever since the advent of the Model T, cars have been a kind of fulcrum between work and play. Usually paid for with wages, they have been both a means and a goal of labor. No-one, however, has ever written a great book or made a great movie about driving to work. For most Americans, the real value in owning a car is what you can do with it when you're not working." Nowhere is this truer than with the ownership of a Jeep. The name Jeep is synonymous with both America and the concept of fourwheelin'. The American nation is blessed with fourwheeling paradises such as Moab, Utah, considered by many to offer the best off-road driving on this planet. If anyone knows for sure, it is the Americans as theirs is the only nation to have been fourwheeling on another planet. It wasn't a Jeep that Apollo 15 took to the moon in 1971 but the Lunar Roving Vehicle (LRV), an expensive custom-built 'wheeler. Astronauts James Irwin and David Scott drove the Boeing-constructed LRV several miles on the moon's surface during the space mission and then left it behind in exactly the way an old flat-fender might be parked up alongside a barn. Closer to home the trend towards the recreational use of trucks was growing ever stronger and had been for several years.

Jeep clubs were founded all over the US; the oldest Jeep Club in the State of Oregon, for example, is the Jolly Jeepers which was founded in 1962. Around this time, Erle Stanley Gardner went off road with the Sareea Al Jamel 4-Wheel Drive Club near Indio, California, in order to describe the growing popularity of recreational four-wheeling in his book *The Desert is Yours*. He described the popular modifications made to Jeeps at that time: "The Jeep will perhaps have a V8 or a six-cylinder motor from a car like a Chevrolet, but it may have an overdrive as well. Then two wheels will be cut in such a way that when the parts are again welded together the space between the rims has been very much widened so that oversize tires can be mounted, thereby giving added traction, particularly in sand. There is simply no limit to what human ingenuity and mechanical ability can accomplish with these things, and, as I soon learned, there is almost no limit to what these things can do." There are limits, of course, and Gardner went on to describe one of the club's light-hearted rituals. "Cliff Gentry, as the latest member to roll his car over and over, has to put the club emblem on his car upside down, and will keep it this way until some other unfortunate member makes a miscalculation; then the new member will take-over with the upside down emblem."

Jeep vehicles were still capable of proving their mettle in more desperate situations. The Pan-American Highway was still incomplete in 1960, so a gap existed between Panama and Colombia. It was known to cartographers as the Darien Gap and to those who lived near it as El Tapon (The Stopper) in Spanish. In 1960 the Darien Sub-committee of the Pan-American Highway Congresses supported an attempt to drive motor vehicles through El Tapon from Chepo, Panama, to Palo de las Letras, Colombia, in the dry season. Two vehicles were used: a Land Rover en route from Canada and a Jeep pickup. The Land Rover was crewed by Englishman Richard Bevis and Australian Terence Whitfield. The Jeep truck was the transport for Otis Imboden, Kip Ross, Amado Arauz, Dr Reina Torres de Arauz and Ilse Abshagen. The first of these were representatives of the Darien Sub-committee and National Geographic Society respectively while the others were a Panamanian cartog-

Right and below: *A 1974 CJ-5 Jeep in export form with right-hand drive. The wheelbase of the CJ-5 was, by this time, 84 inches, but the Jeep was still true to its origins as a working truck.*

Right: *James Lavery's 1976 CJ-7 has been extensively modified for fourwheeling in his home state of Utah.*

Below: *Brochures for the 1962 Kaiser Jeep models; the Jeep Wagoneer and the complete Jeep line.*

rapher, an anthropologist and a European journalist. In addition, the vehicles were accompanied by nine Panamanian woodsmen. The fourwheelers left on February 6 1960 and macheted a way through the jungle, building log bridges over rivers and winching up and down the steepest gradients. The group made its way through Yavisa, Pinojana and El Real and emerged at Palo de las Letras on the Colombian border on May 13 1960 having covered 271 miles. Some days the vehicles

Left: *In order to travel on extreme trails this CJ-7 has been modified to increase ground clearance, suspension travel and axle articulation.*

could only managed half a mile and during the trip there had been 180 creeks and ravines to cross and 125 bridges to build. T. R. Nicholson described the inherent dangers of these bridges in *Wild Roads*: "One such skeleton bridge gave way under the Jeep, which toppled off sideways into the ravine. Luckily the driver was not injured by his ten-foot drop. The Land Rover winched the Jeep upright, then the latter winched itself out of the ravine. Bent bumpers were the sole damage."

It is generally acknowledged that the CJ-5 is the model that spread the word about recreational off-road

driving, especially during the late-sixties and seventies when emphasis was placed on the fact that Jeeps were 'fun' vehicles. The CJ-5 Jeep, introduced in 1955, proved to be a popular model and ensured a healthy profit for its manufacturers. Following the Kaiser-Frazer and Willys-Overland merger the company's car production side was not making a profit, so production of both Kaiser and Willys cars had been abandoned in 1955 in order that the company could concentrate on Jeep production. A spin-off of this policy was the introduction of special Jeeps such as the commercial Forward Control models, the

Above: *The unstoppable Jeep Gladiator in its 1965 form. The 4x4 Jeep truck was available in the Townside form seen here as well as in four other styles.*

Right: *The 1965 Wagoneer was available with a 232 cubic inch in-line six cylinder engine, with the 350 cubic inch Dauntless V8 offered as an option.*

FC-150 and FC-170, and limited edition vehicles such as the 1961 Tuxedo Park. This was a CJ-5 dressed up with chrome hinges, mirror supports and bumper, whitewall tires, and custom wheels and roof. It was intended for golf courses and hotels and stayed in production until 1966, albeit slightly modified with different paint options and upgraded seats. By 1963 the Jeep range included CJ-3B and CJ-5 Jeeps as well as the CJ-6, still available

as the longer wheelbase commercial variant. There were also F-134 model pickups, the FC-series of forward control pickups and the newer, more modern-looking J-series of trucks available in two- and four-wheel drive combinations with payloads of half, three quarter and one ton and a choice of three wheelbases. This range continued for 1964, 1965 and 1966 with minor changes, although the CJ-3B and DJ3A models were discontinued in 1967.

Above: *James Lavery's CJ-7 crossing a gully. Locking differentials are an asset when faced with obstacles such as this because traction is not lost when a wheel is lifted.*

Land Cruiser models. The IH Scout had been unveiled in 1961. The market for four-wheel drive vehicles was growing and although Jeep sales stood up to the increasing competition, they were not rising with the expanding market. Some felt that this was because the Jeep CJ-5 was among the slowest of the 4x4 vehicles. Despite traditional Jeepers' assertions that being fast from 0–60 mph wasn't where a Jeep scored, it did lead to the manufacturer

Below: *A relatively standard CJ-7 in Moab, Utah. The leaf sprung CJ-7 was a competent off-roader even in standard form.*

In 1966 the Ford Bronco had appeared in three styles: roadster pickup, sport utility pickup and wagon. It was intended to compete with both the Jeep and International Harvester's Scout. The Bronco was the first light utility 4x4 built by Ford since its wartime production of the GPW Jeep. Kaiser Jeep was already facing competition from imports such as the British Land Rover and Japanese Datsun and Toyota with their Patrol and

offering a V6 engined CJ-5 from 1966. The V6 was a Buick engine known as the Dauntless with a displacement of 225 cubic inches which produced 155 bhp @ 4000 rpm. By 1968 more than 75% of CJ-5s sold were ordered with the V6 engine option – the Model 8305-A. Kaiser built an engine plant for the production of the V6 engines adjacent to its Jeep Universal assembly plant in Toledo, Ohio. For the remainder of the sixties Jeep

Above and right:
Production of the CJ-7 ran from 1976 until 1986. The CJ-7 was in many ways both a longer wheelbase version of the CJ-5 and the forerunner of the YJ Wrangler models.

continued to develop its range, with the CJ-5 and CJ-6 models being produced alongside other models such as the Jeepster Commando and Wagoneer. Jeep aimed its products at both commercial and recreational users; the pickups were destined to be sold to farmers and the like while machines such as the Commando and Wagoneer were aimed at the embryonic sport utility market. Camper options also appealed to the latter market. There was also a similar division of traditional Jeeps – CJ-6 models were aimed at commercial users (although they did not sell in large numbers) while CJ-5s went to domestic and recreational users. The Jeepster name – last used

Below and right: *The degree to which a Jeep is modified affects its performance in extreme situations. Rick Sparks in his black CJ-7 and the author in a considerably more standard rental CJ-7.*

on a postwar Jeep-like car – was resurrected for 1967 by Kaiser-Jeep and applied to a range of vehicles that included the Jeepster Commando station wagon, pickup and roadster. The grille and front fenders were similar to those of the then current CJ Jeep models while the remainder of the body panels were more unique. Power came from an F-head four cylinder engine displacing 134.2 cubic inches, although a V6 option was also on offer. Manual and automatic transmissions were available and a Dana 20 transfer case provided the four-wheel drive. Production continued until 1973.

Overseas, Jeeps found a place in the various savage civil wars that rocked numerous African nations at this time as European empires were dismantled. Mike Hoare was a mercenary soldier commander during the Congo Rebellion of 1964–65. In his book *Congo Mercenary* he recalled that "the enemy were well concealed and opened fire on Barry's armoured Jeep at thirty yards' range shattering the bulletproof windshield." Jeeps were useful even to irregular armies, Hoare continued. "Force John-John was leading and reported an astounding capture. A brand new Willys Jeep was standing abandoned in the

Below: *Rick Sparks is the owner of Slickrock Jeep and Moab Off Road. He rebuilt this 1986 CJ-7 with a Chevrolet V8 engine and a host of other modifications.*

Right: *The CJ-7 uses 33.12.50.15 Goodyear MT tires on Weld wheels, Rubicon Express springs, Currie spring shackles, Trailmaster shock absorbers and custom axles, all to maximise articulation and traction.*

middle of the road in perfect condition. All it needed was petrol. It was a welcome addition to our fleet." It was a similar story in the Arab-Israeli Six Day War of 1967. An Israeli, Colonel Motta, recalling the fighting around Jerusalem and quoted in Randolph and Winston Churchill's *The Six Day War,* noted that, "'One of our tanks went up in flames at once, as did a number of our reconnaissance Jeeps. We had casualties from the first moment.'"

In 1970 the loss-making Kaiser-Jeep Corporation was purchased by AMC – American Motors Corporation – for approximately $70 million. AMC changed the name of the Jeep-producing part of the organisation to Jeep Corporation but initially only made minor changes to the Jeep models. A special edition Jeepster – the Hurst Jeepster Special – was marketed in 1971. AMC, having moved from being the United States' 131st largest corporation to 75th through the combined sales of AMC and Jeep products totalling $1.2 billion, made a loss of $56.2 million in 1971. This was partially as a result of labor

Below: *Power for the CJ-7 comes from a fuel injected Chevrolet V8 engine.*

relations problems, a downturn in the US economy and the costs of absorbing the Jeep producer. Radical design changes were made to the Jeep lineup for 1972, with new engines for the CJ Jeep range. The F-head four and V6 were dropped and in their place came the 304 cubic inch V8 and the 232 cubic inch in-line six. These necessitated lengthening the wheelbase of both the CJ-5 and CJ-6 by three inches to accommodate them. The extra

Above: *The custom automatic transmission and ARB air locking differentials front and rear help the Jeep in extreme off-road situations.*

length was incorporated into the front fenders so that the overall appearance remained almost the same. New axles, gearbox and transfer case were fitted as were a larger diameter clutch and redesigned pedals. The list of extra cost options was impressive and included freewheeling hubs, power steering, power brakes, limited slip rear differential, additional gauges, heavy duty springs and shock absorbers and a 55 amp alternator. Design

changes to the Jeep range continued for 1973 when the J-series trucks received a wider tailgate and numerous detail improvements. They were also offered with the option of the Quadra-Trac transmission system, a full time four-wheel drive system. Light truck sales tapered off during 1973 due to the 'gas crisis' engendered by the Arab oil embargo. Although this precipitated the trend towards smaller, more economical vehicles in this period,

Above: *The 1978 AMC Jeep range included the J-10 pickup and Wagoneer Station Wagon.*

Left: *The US Mail service used thousands of these DJ-5 models for postal deliveries including this one in Denver, Colorado. Notable features included two-wheel drive, hardtop, sliding doors, parking mirror and a redesigned grille.*

AMC's reaction was to later offer another engine option – the in-line four cylinder 151 cubic inch displacement 'Iron Duke' engine that the company purchased from Pontiac. This option never proved popular and the biggest threat to domestic automakers was from imported compact trucks. In this year Japanese Datsun (later Nissan) and Toyota were selling their Li'l Hustler and Hilux trucks respectively. The CJ models received detail upgrades and the Renegade trim package was first offered as a regular model rather than a limited edition model. The price for base model CJ-5 and CJ-6 Jeeps was less than $100 dollars apart at $3086 and $3176 respectively. Things continued in this vein for both 1974 and 1975 and in the latter year the 400,000th Jeep vehicle since the AMC takeover was built. Things changed for the station wagons in 1974 when the Cherokee made its debut in the growing four-wheel drive market. The Wagoneer became an upmarket prestigious 4x4 while the Cherokee was marketed as a more basic version. Both the vehicles used the same bodyshell but there were numerous detail differences. The Cherokee was fitted with the grille from Jeep's trucks and powered by a 258 cubic inch

vehicle market for several years. It shared many of its features, including engines and transmissions, with the CJ-5 but offered a number of additional features. Foremost among these were wider door openings, more leg room for front and rear seat passengers and an optional molded plastic hardtop. The CJ-7 was the first CJ available with both the turbo Hydra-Matic and Quadra-Trac four-wheel drive system. The standard base model engine

Above: *Greg Klein's Jeep Commando photographed in Lead, South Dakota.*

displacement ohv in-line six, while the Wagoneer used a 360 cubic inch displacement V8 (although there were V8 options for the Cherokee.) Both vehicles had Quadra-Trac four-wheel drive systems but the Wagoneer was only available with automatic transmission.

New for 1976 was another variant of the CJ series Jeeps. It was the CJ-7 with a 93.5 inch wheelbase and seen as one of the most exciting developments in the 4x4

for both the CJ-5 and CJ-7 was an in-line six cylinder of 232 cubic inches displacement, achieved through a bore and stroke of 3.75 x 3.50 inches. It produced 100 bhp @ 3600 rpm. Extra cost optional engines were a 258 cubic inch displacement in-line six and a 304 cubic inch V8. Various trim packages were available including the convenience group package and the Renegade package. Winches and locking rear differentials were also available as factory-fit options, reflecting the off-road use of the Jeep by a significant proportion of buyers.

The next landmark in the development of Jeep's full-size trucks was the announcement of the sporty Honcho package in 1976 for the ongoing J-10 Pickup in short wheelbase form. This vehicle reflected the changing market and competition from Ford and Chevrolet's sport trucks. Available in a choice of six base colors, the

Below: *Production of the Jeep Commando ran from 1967 to 1973; some models were called Jeepsters.*

Below: *CJ-6 production ran from 1956 until 1976. These long wheelbase models were aimed at commercial users. This is a 1974 104-inch wheelbase export model made by AMC.*

Honcho was essentially a dress-up package for the workaday J-10. It included wide 15-inch wheels and tires, gold pinstriping and a rear step bumper. Honcho decals were on the doors, Levi's denim covered the seats and other additions and options included a rollbar and disc brakes. The Honcho package, in this form, remained available for 1977, 1978 and 1979. The stepside pickup bed was a later addition to the Honcho package and was first offered as an option in 1980, AMC referring to it as the Sportside. In this year Jeep sold more than 12,000 J-10 and J-20 pickups.

For the domestic US market the introduction of the CJ-7 coincided with the end of CJ-6 production although it remained available as an export model. Air conditioning and front disc brakes arrived for the CJ-5 and CJ-7 in 1977, the year American Motors celebrated its 75th anniversary. Jeep sales reached a record of 95,718 this year and 25% of the CJ-5 and CJ-7 models sold were ordered with the Renegade trim package. Jeep accounted for 16% of the total US four-wheel drive market at this time. Renault bought 4.7% of AMC stock in March 1978 for $60 million. Into the eighties and the Honcho

package was still available for J-10s as one of a range of trim levels and options that also included the Custom Package, the top of the line Laredo package, the Sportside package, the Honcho Sportside package and options for automatic transmission and a V8 engine.

The trend towards the recreational use of trucks was growing ever stronger. The popularity of mobile homes, camper trailers and truck campers was such that pickup sales were becoming an increasing part of recreational vehicle (RV) sales. Pickups were used to haul trailers and carry camper bodies. To allow Jeep vehicles to gain a

share of this lucrative market, new for 1981 was the CJ-8 Scrambler, a sport utility vehicle that featured CJ-7-type front sheetmetal and a rear load bed on a 104-inch wheelbase chassis. Like the J-10, this four-wheeler was powered by an ohv in-line six cylinder engine of 258 cubic inch displacement. In this form the range of CJ and J-series Jeep products continued almost unchanged, with only detail improvements made annually, until 1984 when the CJ-5 was discontinued. Sales of the CJ-5 had collapsed after the screening of a US TV programme which suggested that the CJ-5 could be susceptible to

Below: AMC Jeep dropped the Gladiator name in 1972 and simply described J-10 and J-20 pickups as Jeep trucks. This is a 1974 Townside model.

Below and left: *A pair of Wyoming registered CJ-5s with factory hardtops; one has a factory fitted V6 engine and an aftermarket snowplough sits through summer waiting for the snows of winter in Lusk, Wyoming.*

stability problems and was easy to roll over. True or not, the damage was done and the CJ-5 went out of production. By this time a total of 603,303 CJ-5s had been built.

The Station Wagon Jeep Wagoneer's basic shape that stretched back to 1963 remained in production until 1983. Over this period it was variously sold as the Cherokee, Cherokee Chief and Grand Wagoneer among others. There were two- and four-door models and numerous engine variations including a 360 cubic inch displacement V8. A range of interior and exterior trim

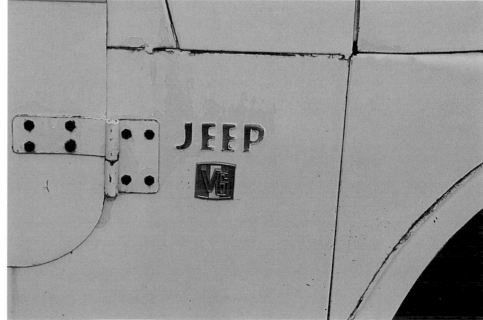

levels was also offered. A new shape Cherokee appeared in 1984, once again considerably modernized and in both two- and four-door forms. The new Wagoneers and Cherokees had been on the drawing boards for five years and were downsized vehicles. They were of a considerably updated design but still had a distinctly Jeep-like appearance about them. An innovative design feature of the new models was the method of construction, termed 'uniframe' by the maker. This incorporated a full length box section steel frame welded to the underside of the floor of the bodyshell and was a departure from the traditional combination of separate chassis and body construction. AMC retained the earlier Wagoneer model as the Grand Wagoneer and offered it with a luxurious level of trim. Sales of both models were strong and in 1984 several US auto magazines including *Petersen's 4-Wheel and Off Road* named the new Jeep Cherokee as 4x4 of

Far Left: *A mildly modified CJ-5 taking part in the Ouray Jeep Jamboree and seen here on a trail that runs up from Telluride, Colorado.*

Right and bottom left: *A Dauntless V6 engined CJ-5 with a factory hardtop at the same event. The towing A-frame, Hi-Lift jack and cowbell are aftermarket fitments.*

The Year. Also new as an option for 1985 Cherokee and Wagoneers models was an in-line four cylinder turbo diesel engine. The engine was an aluminum Renault unit with a Bosch injection system. It displaced 2.1 litres (126 cubic inches) and produced 85 bhp @ 3250 rpm and 132 lbs/ft torque @ 3000 rpm. Sales of the Cherokee and Wagoneer models continued to rise through 1985 to the extent that in the first half of the model year 51,470 vehicles were sold. This equated to a 28% market share of the Sports Utility Vehicle (SUV) market.

In October 1983 216 US Marines were killed when their base in Beirut, Lebanon, was blown up by a suicide bomber. Later the same month US Marines carried out the controversial invasion of Grenada. Contemporary news footage reveals that in both places the USMC were using the late-model variants of the M151. By this time, however, the LTV Missiles and Electronics Group of General Motors' General Division had been awarded a contract for the next generation of military 4x4 by US Army Tank-Automotive Command. It was for the High Mobility Multipurpose Wheeled Vehicle (HMMWV), variously known as the Humvee and Hummer. Manufacture of the new vehicles began in early 1985 and it meant that the US Army's use of the Jeep was effectively over. Times were changing and in January 1986 production of the CJ-7 ceased.

Above: A basic CJ-5 with a factory fitted hardtop, side steps and 15-inch diameter steel wheels. It has also been fitted with freewheeling hubs on the front axle.

Right: A modified CJ-7 Jeep climbing towards the remains of the Tomboy Mine during the Ouray Jeep Jamboree.

AMC Jeep CJ-5

The CJ-5 made its debut in late 1954 as a 1955 model and was closely based on the military MD-M38A1 of the time. During the course of a long production run it was fitted with an in-line four cylinder engine and an optional V6 unit which turned out to be a popular choice with buyers. Almost two decades later the wheelbase was stretched by three inches in order to make sufficient room to fit the American Motors' in-line six cylinder engine. This is a 1974 export model CJ-5 sold in Great Britain – hence its right-hand drive steering configuration – and is original rather than restored.

Specifications

Owner: Unknown
Location: England
Model: CJ-5
Year: 1974
Wheelbase: 84 inches

ENGINE
Model: In-line six
Capacity: 232 cubic inches (3803cc)

TRANSMISSION
Type: Manual 3-speed
Type: Warner T14A
Transfer case: Dana Model 20

SUSPENSION
Front: Semi-elliptical seven leaf springs
Rear: Semi-elliptical five leaf springs

AXLES
Front: Fully floating Dana 30
Rear: Semi-floating Dana 44

BRAKES
Front: 11-inch drums
Rear: 11-inch drums

WHEELS
Type: Kelsey-Hayes steel disc
Size: 6Lx15 inches

TIRES
Type: Goodyear Surburbanite
Size: E78.15 inches

FINISH
Paint: Factory
Color: Trans-Am Red

Above: *A Jeep Cherokee passing the ruins of the Tomboy Mine on the descent from Imogene Pass to Telluride, Colorado.*

"Imogene Pass is the second highest pass in Colorado at 13,114 feet and is one of the most thrilling passes to cross in Colorado. The trail would be impassable most of the summer if not routinely cleared of snow."

COLORADO BACKROADS AND FOUR-WHEEL DRIVE TRAILS. CHARLES A. WELLS. 1998.

WRANGLERS & CHEROKEES

ON NOVEMBER 27 1985 Joseph Cappy, the Executive Vice-president of Operations at American Motor Corporation had announced that the cessation of CJ-7 production was scheduled for the spring of 1986. As a result, few changes were made to the 1985 models for the last few months of production, with standard, Renegade and Laredo models still offered. There was something of a public outcry from loyal customers and Jeep fans about the end of CJ-7 production because the model was still directly linked to the vehicle that 'had won the war.' Cappy did acknowledge the Jeep's legendary status when he said that, "Completion of CJ production will signal an end of a very important era in Jeep history." Despite the announcement, or possibly because of it, Jeep sold in excess of 190,000 Jeeps in the US and Canada in 1985.

AMC had an ace up its sleeve, however, and played it on May 13 1986. It announced the Jeep Wrangler, a all-new model. The Wrangler bore more than a passing resemblance to the old CJ series but was built taking into account a number of outside factors. AMC's engineers knew that a 1986 survey had shown that only 7% of Jeep owners took their vehicles off-road frequently although 80% reported some off-road use. The first figure had been as high as 37% in 1978.

These statistics did not reflect a decline in off-road vehicle usage but the fact that Jeep vehicles were appealing to a wider range of buyers. The new machine had been extensively tested and developed before going into production and was still, at a glance, immediately recognizable as a Jeep, though restyled. The most obvious change was that the radiator grille now featured square headlamps and was partially angled backward. In fact, much of the body tub was like the CJ-7. The sheet metal forward of the firewall including the fenders, hood and grille panel, were all new, and flexible wheel arch extensions were fitted all round. Under the body there were numerous new features including a fuel-injected 2.5 litre in-line four cylinder or 4.2 litre in-line six cylinder engine, five-speed transmission with 'shift on the fly' capability, and power brakes. Leaf spring suspension was retained but set up for a comfortable on-road ride through the inclusion of front and rear track bars and a front stabilizer bar. The interior was comfortable and the hood (on soft top models) and doors were designed to be better fitting and more waterproof. Various trim levels were available including Sahara and Laredo specifications. Of the new model's introduction Jose J. Dedeurwaerder, President and Chief

Left: *Two generations of Jeep Wranglers; the red one is a YJ model while the white one is the newer TJ model.*

Right: *A Jeep making the climb to the summit of the Imogene Pass, more than 13,000 feet above sea level.*

Executive Officer of AMC said, "The Wrangler couldn't come at a better time because interest in Jeep is at an all-time high." The Wrangler was known as the YJ in export markets including Canada where the new Jeeps were assembled at the Bramalea, Ontario, plant. Speaking about the new model AMC's Vice President of Product Engineering and Development, Francois Castaing said that a key objective had been to give the Wrangler good on-road comfort because the buyer profile of the small sport utility vehicle had changed dramatically. Research had shown that 95% of buyers now used their vehicles as everyday transport compared with 17% in 1978, but 80% of owners wanted and used the vehicle's off-road capability.

Right: *The esoteric Californian license plate of a 1999 model TJ Jeep.*

Below: *A YJ Wrangler modified for off-road use. It has been fitted with larger diameter wheels and tires and extended spring shackles are clearly visible.*

Behind the public face of Jeep sales there had been considerable activity. In November 1986 it became known that Chrysler was interested in acquiring AMC who were in serious difficulties and had been for some time. Renault by now owned 46% of AMC stock and it too was in trouble; the new Renault models had not sold as well as expected in the US. Between 1980 and 1984 AMC lost $622 million, while Renault lost $1.79 billion and $1.56 billion in 1984 and 1985 respectively. Renault was making cutbacks in France and putting money into what was perceived as a lost cause in the US. This led to considerable unrest in France and the assassination of Renault's Chairman

Left: *A TJ Jeep making a flamboyant stream crossing. The winch is an aftermarket fitment while Dick Cepek is an established aftermarket parts manufacturer.*

Far Left: *A modified YJ Wrangler climbing from Ouray towards the summit of Imogene Pass.*

Left: *Wind in the hair motoring; one of the reasons that Jeeping is so enjoyable is that Jeep manufacturers have retained the folding soft top roof.*

Below: *The recent range of Jeep station wagons such as Cherokees are still capable off-road vehicles.*

Georges Besse on November 17 1986. Clearly Renault had to withdraw from the US. Behind the scenes Chrysler worked out a deal to acquire additional manufacturing capability and part of the growing recreational 4x4 market by buying Renault's AMC stock. The new generation Jeeps – Wranglers and Cherokees – would be produced by Chrysler's Jeep Eagle Division. By 1989 the Wrangler range included the base model, the S, the Sahara, the Laredo and, for the first time, the Islander. The Islander version of the Wrangler was not as luxuriously appointed as the Laredo but boasted more extras than the base and S models, including charcoal-colored carpet, upholstery, soft top and spare wheel cover. Special Islander body colors included Malibu Yellow, Pearl White, Pacific Blue and Red. Such schemes enhanced the appeal of the Jeep to the extent that Don-A-Vee Jeep, an

established dealer from Bellflower, California, sold 2,453 Jeeps during 1989. By 1991 typical Wrangler buyers were single, male, 29-years-olds, with an average income of $34,000.

Alongside the four-wheel drive versions of the Cherokee and Wagoneer AMC offered a number of two-wheel drive vehicles including the Cherokee Pioneer sportwagon. Pioneer was one of the levels of trim specification that also included base, Chief and Laredo. The Pioneer was immediately above base level and therefore a relatively basic machine which included painted steel wheels fitted with radial tires. From 1986 onwards Jeep vehicles were covered by a 12 month/12,000 mile warranty, three-year corrosion warranty and the engine and major powertrain components were covered for 24 months/24,000 miles. The 1987 models were announced in the fall of 1986 – the Grand Wagoneer still soldiered on with the early-style bodyshell and upgrades were largely cosmetic. The standard engine was a 360 cubic inch (5.9 litre) V8 and mechanically the vehicle was not changed. It still had servo-assisted disc brakes, PAS and power locks and 'English Walnut' woodgrain trim was used on the exterior along with new Grand Wagoneer and

Right: *Old and new; a classic V6 CJ-5 follows a Cherokee that is at least two decades younger on a Colorado trail at the Jeep Jamboree.*

Below: *The newest generation of Jeep station wagons is the Grand Cherokee. It is designed to mix highway comfort and off-pavement ability.*

Left: *Jeep-sponsored Jeep Jamborees attract a wide range of Jeep products ranging from this stock Cherokee to more modified Jeeps.*

Above: *A Grand Cherokee on one of the scenic county maintained four-wheel drive trails in the San Juan mountains.*

V8 badges. Also fitted with 'English Walnut' woodgrain panels was the 1987 Jeep Wagoneer Limited available as a two- and four-door model. The standard engines were an in-line six and an in-line four respectively. Optional engines included the six cylinder – in vehicles where it was not standard – and the Renault turbo-diesel. The latter was not available in California but was one of the vehicle's assets when it was marketed in Europe. All versions of the Wagoneer and Cherokee models were available for 1987 with an optional 241.6 cubic inch (3.96 litre) in-line six cylinder fuel-injected engine that ensured a 0–60 mph time of less than ten seconds. It produced 173 bhp @ 4500 rpm and 220 lbs/ft torque @ 3000 rpm. Performance like this ensured the popularity of SUVs. The

127

Right: *Joe Doyle from Oakforest, Illinois driving his modified YJ Wrangler on a section of the Porcupine Rim trail in Moab, Utah.*

Left: *Rudy Martinez from Chicago, Illinois, eases his YJ Wrangler up a rockstep obstacle on the same trail.*

Below: *The passenger's view through the windshield of a CJ-7 on the Porcupine Rim trail. It is passable for 4x4s from Sand Flats Road to Jackass Canyon.*

Cherokee Chief remained part of the 1987 lineup although the makers shifted the emphasis of their range slightly for 1988. The Wagoneer was only offered as the Wagoneer Limited while the Cherokee Limited was offered in both two- and four-door forms. The turbo-diesel engine option was dropped and the six cylinder engine became standard across much of the range. A comprehensive list of optional extras was available for the Cherokee including heavy duty cooling systems, air conditioning, a cold climate package, an off-road package, various towing packages, bumper guards and skid plates. Numerous smaller items were also on offer such as tinted windows, power seats, sunroofs, external spare tire carrier, rear window wipers, map lights and courtesy lights. Jeep had had three successive record sales years in the years up to 1988 and in that year the Cherokee was the best-selling 4x4 in America's top ten Jeep dealers. The old-

style V8 Grand Wagoneer was last produced during 1991 and less than 1,600 were made in that year. Despite this the vehicle had had a production run of 28 years and was still clearly recognizable as the same vehicle launched in 1963. It had, of course, been progressively moved upmarket, initially to make room for the new shape Cherokees and Wagoneers, but later to ensure that AMC offered a SUV for every niche within the burgeoning four-wheel drive market. The Wagoneer name disappeared from the range of Jeep products in 1992. From 1993 onwards, the Grand Cherokee was redesigned as a station wagon.

The 1987 model J-10 pickups had, as usual, been announced in the fall of the year previous and, with the

Left: *Dan Mick leads groups of four-wheel drive vehicles around the trails of Moab's Canyon Country in this modified YJ Wrangler Jeep.*

Right: *The interior of Rick Sparks' Chevrolet V8 powered 1986 CJ-7. The rollcage is a useful safety feature on extreme trails.*

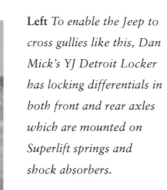

Left *To enable the Jeep to cross gullies like this, Dan Mick's YJ Detroit Locker has locking differentials in both front and rear axles which are mounted on Superlift springs and shock absorbers.*

Below: *For increased strength in this sort of situation, the Jeep has been fitted with axles custom built by Currie. They are based around the so-called Ford 9-inch unit.*

exception of paint colors, were almost unchanged from 1986. One reason for this was that this was to be the last year for both the J-10 and J-20 full-size pickups. The 258 cubic inch displacement in-line six cylinder engine was the standard engine in the J-10 although a V8 option remained available and was standard in the J-20. Both pickups were offered in base and Pioneer trim levels. The Jeep Comanche pickup shared much of its front sheetmetal with the new style Jeep Cherokee XJ station wagon. The Comanche, a downsized truck designed to compete head on with the Japanese imports, was derived from the Cherokee and incorporated the same unitized body and chassis construction. It was available in both 4x2 and 4x4 forms on a 120-inch wheelbase chassis. It was powered by an in-line four cylinder engine and a turbo-diesel engine was listed as an option. The first 119.6-inch wheelbase models were available in 1986 and the range was widened for 1987. A shorter wheelbase version, the Model 64, measuring 113 inches between the axles, was offered, as was an optional six

cylinder engine in place of the four. There were four trim levels offered although the Laredo was exclusive to the long wheelbase Model 66 and the Chief to the short version. Base and Pioneer were available on both. The longer pickup bed made the long wheelbase version of the pickup more useful to commercial operators but at the expense of off-road performance – the longer rear overhang decreased the vehicle's departure angle considerably. The overhang measured 47.1 inches, giving a departure angle of 24.8 degrees compared with the short version's overhang of 38.7 inches and departure angle of 30.1 degrees. Comanche trucks had considerable off-road racing success in the late-eighties. In 1987 and 1988 the Archer Brothers team won the Manufacturers Championship with 2.5 litre-engined Comanches. Jeep Comanche trucks also won the HDRA/SCORE Off Road Racing Series Manufacturers Championship in both 1987 and '88. Also in 1988 the Comanche had the best record of any domestic US truck in the Mickey

Above: *The main difference between YJ and TJ Jeeps is that the TJ uses coil springs in its suspension.*

Right: *At a glance there doesn't appear to be much room under the hood of a TJ Wrangler.*

Far right: *Phil Howell's TJ Jeep has been extensively modified for use on trails such as those around Moab, Utah.*

Thompson Stadium Racing Series but that claim does acknowledge the imported competition from the likes of Toyota. Comanche production was halted in 1992.

In 1997 the YJ Wrangler with its distinctive rectangular headlights was superseded by the TJ model. At a glance the most obvious change was that the Jeep's design had reverted to circular headlights. The biggest change, however, was hidden underneath the slightly redesigned sheetmetal. The Jeep Wrangler now featured coil spring suspension in place of the traditional fore and aft leaf springs that had endured since the Willys Quad. The choice of engines and transmissions remained unchanged; in-line four and six cylinders coupled to five-speed manual and three-speed automatic transmissions. The wheelbase of the TJ Wrangler remained unchanged from that of the CJ-7, as had the YJ Wrangler and, like the CJ-7, the TJ Wrangler was constructed around a separate steel ladder chassis and steel body tub unlike the 'unitized' Cherokee models. Although intended to comply with

Left: *Electric winches such as the Warn unit on this TJ are an essential tool for self recovery on difficult trails.*

Bottom left: *Aggressive, large diameter tires such these 35.14.50.15 Super Swampers on Phil Howell's TJ enhance ground clearance and traction off-road.*

Right: *Easier trails such as this one abound in the Canyonlands and Arches National Parks in the vicinity of Moab.*

Left: *The Lion's Back is a noted Utah landmark near Moab. Seen here descending it are Kevin Hawkins and Dan Mick in a CJ-2A and a YJ Wrangler respectively.*

Right: *Two generations of modified Jeeps; Rick Sparks' CJ-7 and Dan Mick's YJ Wrangler.*

modern legislation and market demands the redesign did not detract from the now classic styling of the basic, open-top Jeep.

And ultimately it was the basic, open-top Jeep that made the legend. Over fifty years earlier, in *The Brass Ring*, Bill Mauldin wrote, "While Anna might have had some reservations about me at first, she was crazy about my Jeep. She liked the windshield down; since the weather had turned balmy I didn't mind. For the next few weeks we travelled all over northern Italy with her rump in the right hand seat, her forepaws on the hood, and her ears twitching in the wind." In the way Mauldin understood and respected the GIs of World War Two, he also understood Jeeps and Jeeping. Mauldin, the man who was able to refer to one of World War Two's greatest photographers, Robert Capa, as 'Bob,' deserves the last word. "We found the best way to liberate a place is in your own Jeep. As far as the girls were concerned we were Don Juan and Casanova in a Ferrari."

Custom Rockcrawler CJ-2A

The early Jeeps pioneered the mass market for four-wheel drive vehicles and blazed the trail for recreational 'fourwheeling,' which brings us to the CJ2A on these pages. Kevin Hawkins built this example, the basis of which is a 1948 CJ2A body tub and chassis. The stock chassis was beefed up and had the custom rollcage welded to it in eight places. The refurbished steel body tub was refitted to the chassis and everything else reconstructed around it. This flatfender may have passed the half century since it rolled off the Toledo line but in its present incarnation it's as up-to-date as anything that can be found on Moab's nastiest trails.

Specifications

Owner: Kevin Hawkins
Location: Salt Lake City, Utah
Model: CJ-2A
Year: 1948
Wheelbase: 80 inches

ENGINE
Model: Buick V6
Capacity: 225 cubic inches (3687cc)

TRANSMISSION
Type: Automatic
Model: Chevrolet TH350
Transfer case: Dana Model 18

SUSPENSION
Front: Semi-elliptical leaf springs
Rear: Quarter-elliptical leaf springs

AXLES
Front: Currie Dana 44/Detroit Locker
Rear: Currie Dana 44/Detroit Locker

BRAKES
Front: Disc
Rear: Disc

WHEELS
Type: Alloy with bead-locks
Size: 8x15 inches

TIRES
Type: Goodyear MT
Size: 35.12.50.15 inches

FINISH
Paint: Custom
Color: Teal Blue

GLOSSARY

AMC American Motors Corporation

CID Cubic Inch Displacement

CJ Civilian Jeep

CO Commanding Officer

CP Command Post

DOA Department of Agriculture

Deuce-and-a-half US 2.5 ton 6x6 truck

Dogface WWII slang for G.I.

DUKW amphibious deuce and a half

Dust-off Medevac helicopter

ETO European Theater of Operations

Fourwheeler Slang for 4x4 vehicle

GPA Amphibious Jeep

GPW Ford-manufactured Willys Jeep

Grunt Vietnam War slang for G.I.

Huey Bell HU-1E helicopter

KSCB Khe Sahn Combat Base

LBJ President Lyndon Baines Johnson

LCpl Lance Corporal

LRDG Long Range Desert Group

LRV Lunar Roving Vehicle

MB Standardised Willys military Jeep

MUTT Military Utility Tactical Truck

NDRC National Defense Research Committee

NEKAF Netherlands Kaiser Factory

NVA North Vietnamese Army

Petrol English name for Gasoline

PPA Popski's Private Army

PTO Pacific Theater of Operations

PTO Power Take Off

SAS Special Air Service

Six-by Deuce-and-a-half

SSW South South-West

SUV Sport Utility Vehicle

UCLA University College of Los Angeles

UK United Kingdom

USMC United States Marine Corps

USN United States Navy

VD Venereal Disease

'Wheeler' Slang for 4x4 vehicle, as fourwheeler

YJ Wrangler Jeep

BIBLIOGRAPHY

Allen, Col. Robert S.
Patton's Third US Army. Lucky Forward
Vanguard Press Inc 1947

Barbey, Daniel and Boucher, Henri
New York Patagonie ou 35,000 km en Jeep
J. Peyronnet and Cie 1950

Carlin, Ben
Half Safe
Andre Deutsch 1955

Carlin, Ben
The Other Half of Half Safe
Guildford Grammar School Foundation Inc
1995

Ceurvorst, Joe
Africa in a Jeep
Staples Press Ltd 1956
(*L'Afrique en Jeep*
Hatier-Boivin)

Churchill, Randolph S. and Winston S.
The Six Day War
William Heinemann Ltd 1967

Cowles, Virginia
The Phantom Major
Collins 1958

Cullen, Jim
*Born in the USA. Bruce Springsteen and the
American Tradition*
Harper Collins Publishers Inc 1997

Currey, Cecil B.
Follow Me and Die
Stein and Day Inc 1984

Eberhart, Perry
*Guide to the Colorado Ghost Towns and
Mining Camps*
Sage Books 1959

Gardner, Erle Stanley
Hunting the Desert Whale
Jarrolds (London) Ltd 1961

Gardner, Erle Stanley
The Desert is Yours
Jarrolds (London) Ltd 1966

Hammel, Eric
The Siege of Khe Sahn: An Oral History
Crown Publishers Inc 1989

Harvey, Frank
Air War – Vietnam
Bantam Books Inc 1967

Hoare, Mike
Congo Mercenary
Robert Hale Ltd 1967

Hoyt, Edwin P.
The Bloody Road to Panmunjon
Stein and Day 1985

Jones, James
WWII
Leo Cooper Ltd 1975

Leinbaugh, Harold P. and John D. Campbell
The Men of Company K
William Morrow and Co 1985

Longmate, Norman
The G.I.s. The Americans in Britain
Hutchinson and Co (publishers) Ltd 1975

Marshall, General George C.
*Report on the Army July 1, 1939 to June 30,
1943*
The Infantry Journal 1943

Mason, Robert.
Chickenhawk
Corgi Books 1983

Mauldin, Bill
Up Front
Henry Holt and Co Inc 1945

Mauldin, Bill
The Brass Ring
W. W. Norton & Co Inc 1971

McCauley, Alvan
Defense on the Assembly Line
Popular Mechanics magazine August 1941

Michael, Marjorie
I Married a Hunter
Odhams 1957

Nicholson, T.R.
Wild Roads
Jarrolds Publishers (London) Ltd. 1969

Peniakoff, Vladimir
Private Army
Jonathan Cape 1950

Pyle, Ernie
Here Is Your War
Henry Holt and Company Inc 1943

Rogers, Dorothy
Jeopardy and a Jeep
Richard R. Smith 1957

Schreider, Frank and Helen
*La Tortuga. An amphibious journey from
Alaska to Tierra Del Fuego*
Secker and Warburg 1957.

Stettinius Jr. Edward R.
Lend-Lease. Weapon for Victory
Penguin Books 1944

Van Duyne, Schuyler
*From Cook Stoves to Tanks ... They roll from
the automobile factories*
Popular Science Magazine August 1941

Wells, A. Wade
Hail to the Jeep
Harper and Brothers 1946

Wells, Charles A.
Colorado Backroads & 4-Wheel Drive Trails
Funtreks Inc. 1998

Zumbro, Ralph
Tank Sergeant
Pocket Books, Simon and Schuster Inc 1988